FELICIA CARTRIGHT

AND THE CASE OF THE
MISSING SIDEBOARD

Felicia   Joan

FELICIA CARTRIGHT

AND THE CASE OF THE
MISSING SIDEBOARD

BERNARD PALMER

Aneko Press *Youth*

www.anekopress.com

Aneko Press, Life Sentence Publishing, and our logos are trademarks of Life Sentence Publishing, Inc.
203 E. Birch Street
P.O. Box 652
Abbotsford, WI 54405

JUVENILE FICTION / Religious / Christian / Action & Adventure

Paperback ISBN: 979-8-88936-284-5

eBook ISBN: 979-8-88936-285-2

10 9 8 7 6 5 4 3 2 1

Available where books are sold

CONTENTS

CHAPTER I

THE MISSING SIDEBOARD

Felicia Cartright brushed her soft blond hair from her face with a nervous gesture and leaned forward eagerly to show the magazine to Miss Duncan, the Dean at Wellington School for Girls.

"But don't you see, Miss Duncan," she said, her voice quivering with excitement, "the sideboard that Miss Grainger left to the school could be the one referred to in this article? She traced her ancestry back to the Revolution and always boasted that she had a close relative who had been killed in the opening days of battle."

Her companions stepped closer to the desk. There was Joan Bailey, tall and slender as a willow, who was more at home on the tennis court than in class, and Gretchen Armour, a dainty little brunette, who worked calculus for recreation.

Miss Duncan picked up the magazine and scanned

the article hurriedly, reading about the sideboard, which was a large, old-fashioned chest of drawers built something like a buffet.

"'It has long been suspected,'" she read aloud, "'that Abner Parker, who was killed in a skirmish outside Boston in the opening weeks of the Revolution, built not one, but two of his world-famous sideboards. The recent discovery of his ledger reveals that to be true. One sideboard has been on display at a Boston museum since its purchase for more than $40,000 in 1954. The other was, according to the ledger, sold to one Jonas C. Parker, in exchange for two pigs and a suckling calf on June 2, 1772. Since that time nothing has been heard of it. It is probably gathering dust in somebody's attic. . . .'"

All three girls were studying Miss Duncan intently. She put aside the magazine and pursed her lips.

"Miss Grainger's mother's maiden name was Parker," Felicia went on. "And she did value the sideboard highly. The other furniture was bequeathed generally. I'm just positive that it's the Parker sideboard."

The dean of women smiled tolerantly, her severe, gaunt little face softening a bit. It wasn't often that the girls at Wellington saw her smile.

"It is true that Miss Grainger's mother was a Parker," she admitted. "But that is hardly proof that the sideboard she left the school was made by Abner Parker, especially since her personal effects have been gone over painstakingly, and no sign of it has been found."

"But she must have had it," Joan put in. "She mentioned it specifically in her will."

Miss Duncan opened her desk and took out a thick envelope.

"You know, of course," she continued, "that the board of directors sent Mr. Wharton to Maine to look into the matter. He came back with the information that he doubted whether the sideboard left to Wellington even existed. And if it did, he reported that he had serious doubts that it would be of special value. There was nothing else among Miss Grainger's possessions of more than nominal value."

Felicia sat back, struggling vainly to mask her disappointment. She was a small girl with gentle blue eyes and dainty features; a happy, lively girl with a smile that had a way of toying playfully with the corners of her mouth. According to the way the guys flocked around her when they came over from nearby Barrington College, she was one of the most popular girls at Wellington. But now she was crestfallen.

"When I learned why you girls wanted to see me this morning," Miss Duncan went on, "I went to Mrs. Dillman and secured permission to show you this letter and the copy of the will, which the attorney sent to us."

She handed the papers to Joan. "Would you please read the portions we have marked in red, Miss Bailey?"

Laughing a little, nervously, Joan took the envelope and opened it. She was taller than Felicia, with short, black hair and a quick, open, decisive manner that somehow made her popular, even though her grades often left something to be desired.

"'The sideboard mentioned in the will, which evidently Miss Grainger felt to be quite valuable, although she does not state why, has been given to the Wellington School for Girls. Unfortunately, we have been unable to find either the sideboard or the papers which would prove its value, although we have made an extensive search for both. . . .'" Joan looked up. "Is that all you wanted me to read?" she asked.

The school official nodded, allowing a smile to rest briefly on her face.

"On the second page he calls attention to the section of the will that says the school must claim the sideboard within six months of the date of the official notice of the bequest, or it reverts to her cousin, Mrs. Clarissa Ewing. Of course," she laughed, "since the sideboard can't even be found, that provision is of very little importance."

It was Gretchen who picked up the little calendar on Miss Duncan's desk and checked the months and the days rapidly. Gretchen had come to Wellington on a scholarship and had spent the last three years living up to it. Her straight A's were the pride of the school, and her help had saved Joan, more than once, from "the high executioner's ax," come exam time.

"There are only two weeks left in the allotted six months," she said decisively. "That means that anything that is done is going to have to be done immediately."

Joan Bailey leaned back in her chair with obvious lack of interest.

"If you ask me," she said impudently, "the old gal was a little batty. I think that's what Miss Duncan is trying to tell us."

Felicia picked up the obscure little antique fancier's magazine and began to read the account of the sideboard again.

Miss Duncan's nose wrinkled disapprovingly at Joan.

"I wouldn't want you to think that, Miss Bailey," she protested. "I would have you know that Miss Grainger was one of our most faithful alumni. She loved Wellington and everything that the school stands for. But she was very old and, I understand, quite childish. We went over this matter at great length and concluded, sorrowfully, I can assure you, that Miss Grainger must have imagined that she had had that sideboard. The very fact that she descended from the famous Abner Parker could have well caused her to have daydreams."

She folded the papers again and placed them back in the envelope.

"So, while we appreciate the interest you girls have shown in the matter, we feel that we have taken the more realistic course of action."

Joan and Gretchen turned to go, reluctantly, but Felicia said, "I know that. But the thing that disturbs me is the fact that the rest of the will is both practical and sound. There isn't anything in it that would make us think that Miss Grainger was a–a little eccentric, is there?"

Miss Duncan scowled.

"Our decision has been made, Miss Cartright. We considered the matter very carefully."

"I think we ought to go up to Maine," Joan said, tossing her head. "We could go from farmhouse to farmhouse saying, 'Please may I come in and see if you have a spare sideboard? It's just a little old thing worth hundreds of thousands of dollars.'"

Even Miss Duncan permitted herself to smile a little, although it was done grudgingly.

"You certainly have my permission to use the coming holiday for that if you wish," she said, rising. "It might satisfy your curiosity."

Then she turned significantly to Joan. "Providing, of course, that you have an acceptable grade on your tests and don't have to spend the time studying."

"Why don't you talk to Gretchen about that too?" Joan smiled.

Felicia looked over at Joan and Gretchen quickly.

"We have been talking about going up there," she said, "if you think it would be all right."

"It will be quite all right with us," Miss Duncan said firmly. "Although, I hardly need to add that it will also be a waste of time."

Back in their room, when the interview with Miss Duncan was over, Joan flopped wearily on the bed.

"I don't know why I ever let you two talk me into going up to Maine to look for a sideboard that doesn't exist," she said. "Here I had everything planned for a perfectly wonderful holiday. Now we're going to spend those two gorgeous weeks up in the Maine woods to poke around in the dust of old attics."

"You were the one who mentioned it to us," Gretchen said, "and to Miss Duncan too, if I remember correctly."

"It's going to be fun," Felicia told them. "And I just know that sideboard exists. Miss Grainger wasn't the kind of woman to make up something like that. She left that sideboard to the school because it's something very valuable. I'm convinced that it's a genuine Parker."

"Genuine Parker or not," Joan said disgustedly, as she threw her feet over the side of the bed and sat up, "that old gal was off her rocker. Did you ever read what her yearbook has to say about her? Gretchen dug this out of the library this morning. It's the yearbook of her graduating class."

She went over to the desk and opened the thin

volume to a picture of a sweet-faced, young lady in white lace. Although it had been taken when she was a young girl, they would still have recognized her. She had the same quiet look about her, the same dignity that set her apart from any of the other alumni who came back to visit at Wellington.

"Just listen to this," Joan said, reading, "'Miss Martha Grainger, whose sterling Christian character is an inspiration to all of us. Her favorite book is the Bible, and her favorite pastime is talking to her classmates about Christ. There are those who will spend eternity with the Lord because they knew Martha Grainger.'"

Joan closed the book in disgust.

"As crazy as a loon," she announced.

Gretchen smiled tolerantly.

"That's Martha Grainger, all right," she said. "My mother introduced her to me a long time ago. Before I had known her fifteen minutes, she began to talk to me about my soul."

Joan Bailey's face darkened. "Nobody talks to Bailey about her soul," she said firmly. "I'm going to rule my own life without any interference from anybody."

Felicia felt the color come up into her cheeks and, almost involuntarily, she turned away. A few short months ago she had felt the same as Gretchen and Joan about Christian things but–

She had planned to tell them about her newly

found faith when school convened that September. She had been going to church and Sunday school with some degree of regularity, ever since her grade school days, but she had never really thought much about Christ in a vital, personal way until those two weeks at camp.

There she had heard, for the first time, what it really meant to be a Christian. She saw that Christ had died for her sins and that she was headed for a lost eternity unless she made her decision to follow Him.

Throughout the camping period she had fought doggedly against the dictates of her heart. The last night there, just as she began to relax a little, thinking the battle against Christ had been won, the message swept aside, with brutal honesty she faced the tinsel and sham with which she wrapped her objections. Her very soul was left raw and bleeding until she gave in and turned her heart and life over to Him.

She had decided, almost immediately, that she would have to tell the girls at school about her newly found faith. And especially Joan and Gretchen. The three of them had been inseparable since the first day they came to Wellington. Indeed, she had lain awake nights thinking about what she would say.

She had decided what Bible verses she would quote, what examples she would give, and how she would use her own testimony. She had decided just how she would bring up the subject, first to Joan, and then to Gretchen.

For days before going back to school she had prayed diligently about the matter. But it had been so much easier to plan than to do. Joan was brash and cynical and so giddy at times that

there was no talking seriously with her. Gretchen, on the other hand, was so intellectual that she knew everything about everything. She swallowed every theory and wild speculation that science offered and considered herself too intellectual to accept the Bible as truth and herself as a sinner. Felicia tried a dozen times to talk to them, but somehow, she couldn't manage to talk to them of Christ.

There had been one opportunity the second week after school had started, but it only lasted for a moment. Joan and Gretchen noticed that she hadn't taken in the round of parties and dances they had been in the habit of attending and had been going to church regularly on Sundays.

"You seem so different since you came back to school this fall, Felicia," Gretchen had observed, "that we hardly know you. What's come over you, anyway?"

Felicia hesitated a moment. The color dotted her cheeks, and she felt a quick spasm of fear. Hurriedly she prayed for guidance.

"What's the matter?" Joan had asked her then. "Are you in love?"

One of the other girls had come up just then.

"Did I hear somebody say something about love?"

she asked, laughing. "I thought I was the only one who fell in love every summer. Don't tell me that it happened to you too, Felicia."

Felicia Cartright's heart sank. If anybody else in the dormitory had come up just then, she could have continued. But not with Betsy Ann.

Everybody laughed and began to chide her. She had blushed daintily. Just enough to make them think that she had met someone during the summer.

And so the chance to tell them that she had given her heart to the Lord Jesus was gone.

CHAPTER 2

AT THE OLD HOMESTEAD

The girls had their tests at Wellington the first of the following week, and on Thursday morning they were ready to leave. They went to Maine in Joan's convertible, the gift of an overindulgent grandfather.

"I don't know why I ever let you talk me into a thing like this, Felicia," Joan said as they drove along the tree-lined highway toward southern Maine. "I'm missing two good dances and half a dozen parties at home just to come up here and look for a piece of furniture that probably doesn't even exist."

"I feel a little ridiculous myself," Gretchen said. "If the school authorities couldn't find this sideboard, it seems rather foolish for us to think that we can."

"Just you wait," Felicia told them with a confidence that she did not feel. She had been hoping, prayerfully, that this would be an opportunity for her to talk to them about the Lord Jesus. For the best part of the week, she would be alone with them.

"Well!" Joan said some six or seven hours later, as they turned off the main highway at Farmington, Maine, and sped out into the rocky hills toward the old Grainger place. "We'll soon see whether there's anything to this or not. Maybe we can get back in time for the parties, after all. Or," she looked over at Felicia and laughed, "perhaps Felicia will get tired of this, and the two of you can go home with me in time for all of them. That would be the best idea."

"I'm sure that it would be just as profitable," Gretchen added.

Felicia looked at the map.

"I think we turn here," she said. "The man at the station said that they lived in the second three-story house on the left-hand side of the road."

Joan slowed down a little. There to the left was a great three-story house of another era, with a barn and servants' quarters attached. It was a massive, well-built house with high, narrow windows and an air of great stability.

The house itself was large enough, but with the barn and implement shed attached, it stretched along the lane like some ancient mansion.

"The place is dark," Gretchen said, shuddering. "I don't believe there's anybody at home."

"There's a light at the back," Joan said, turning in. "On the first floor."

"You don't mean that we're going to stay here, do you?" Gretchen asked. "It makes the shivers run up my spine just to look at it."

"We'll know about that in a minute," Joan answered. She stopped the car and got out.

"Do you want us to go to the door with you?" Felicia asked.

"If I need your help, I'll call on you," and Joan laughed.

A spindling, sharp-faced woman with piercing black eyes and gray-streaked hair came to the door in answer to Joan's knock. She opened it a crack, suspiciously, and peered out, her lips pursed narrowly.

"What do you want?" she asked, her voice thin and shrill. "We're almost ready for bed."

"Good evening," Joan said evenly. "Miss Duncan wrote you about our coming. We were to get a room for a few days."

The door opened a little wider.

"We got no letter from anybody."

Joan stood there a moment.

"But you're Mrs. Herman Ewing, aren't you?" she asked. "And this is the old Grainger place, isn't it?"

"What if it is?" the woman retorted. She took a step back and moved as though to close the door.

"We had a short vacation at school," Joan explained, "and decided that we'd like to come up here to spend part of it. Miss Duncan was going to write and get a room for us."

Herman Ewing, who had been sitting at the kitchen table, got up and started toward his wife.

"What is it, Clarissa?" he asked. "What do they want?"

She turned and scowled but did not answer him.

"What do you girls want to do way out here in the country?" she asked. "Why don't you get a room nearer town?"

"Well," Joan said looking about significantly, "to tell you the truth, we're interested in antiques. That's why we like to go out into the country like this."

Without saying so, she made it sound as though they spent most of their spare time searching for antiques. Felicia winced as she heard her lie so smoothly.

"Antiques?" Mrs. Ewing echoed, brightening. "Do you buy them?"

"If we find something we like."

The woman's whole manner changed.

"Won't you come in, my dear?" she asked. "And have your friends come in too. You must be tired if you've driven far."

She paused momentarily.

"It so happens," she said, "that we have quite a number of choice antiques that I'm certain you might be interested in. You see, my dear cousin passed on a few months ago, and my husband and I have the unpleasant task of managing her affairs."

Joan got Felicia and Gretchen and introduced them to the Ewings.

"It's so nice to have you girls here," Clarissa Ewing said, smiling crookedly as she got her light shawl and threw it about her shoulders. "I'll take you out and show you a room we have. It's out in the servants' quarters over the implement shed, but it's a large room and clean. I'm sure you'll like it. You see, we only opened three rooms in the house."

"As a matter of fact," her husband said, looking up from his book, "this place gives us the creeps. Just as soon as we get rid of this junk, we're clearing out of here."

"Herman!" Clarissa scolded. "You know that the pieces of furniture in this magnificent old house are real treasures."

She turned to Joan and smiled tolerantly. "You know how some men are when it comes to antiques," she said. "Herman thinks that if anything is more than ten years old, it's junk."

The girls got their bags and followed Clarissa Ewing out to the servants' quarters and up the steep stairs to their room.

"We started cleaning out here," the woman explained. "And it just so happens that we have these rooms ready. Otherwise, we'd be very happy to put you up in the house. But I'm certain that you'll find it comfortable."

The other two girls walked across the room and

set their bags down, but Felicia stood for a moment or two, looking about hungrily.

"I'm sure you'll find our place here a real treasure house," Mrs. Ewing continued. "And Herman and I are so anxious to get things settled that we are willing to sacrifice everything."

She set the old-fashioned kerosene lamp on the great walnut dresser and showed the girls the clothes closet and the bath down the hall.

"My cousin Martha didn't bring electricity out here, only into the three rooms where Herman and I are living. She was a little strange, the poor dear."

"I'm sure that she was," Joan answered cryptically.

For a moment, Mrs. Ewing eyed her, a question in her face. But she said nothing. Instead, she turned to Felicia and Gretchen.

"I suppose you girls haven't had anything to eat yet this evening," she said. "If you wish to come down in about half an hour or so, I'll have something ready for you. It won't be much at this hour, but it will tide you over until tomorrow."

"That would be fine," Felicia answered. "It has been quite a while since we ate."

Mrs. Ewing left them, and the girls walked slowly around the room, staring.

"Just look at this room," Felicia exclaimed breathlessly. "That chair and that old clock on the wall."

"And that two-inch mattress on the bed," Joan

retorted, smiling. "This isn't my idea of a place to come for a rest."

But Felicia scarcely heard her.

"Everything is just the way it was when Miss Grainger was a little girl. I don't think they've changed a thing."

"I have no doubt about it," Joan said, sitting down on the straight, high-backed chair with a groan. "Give me a nice, overstuffed chair and a lamp that works with a switch every time. I guess I'm just a modern girl."

Gretchen went to the door and looked down the long, dark hall.

"You know," she said, shivering, "it gives me the chills to think of staying in a room like this with so many empty rooms around us; and so far from where the Ewings will be sleeping."

"Yes," Joan answered, "there's plenty of room for ghosts to rattle around in this house."

Herman Ewing soon called the girls to dinner. He was as thin and waspish as his wife, with a faint suggestion of a mustache on his upper lip and a double handful of gray hair sprinkled across his balding head.

"We surely are glad to have you girls spend a few days with us," he said. "Clarissa and I don't have much company. We get sort of lonesome all by ourselves." He pushed past them to open the door. "But we're not going to be stuck out here very long. Just as soon as we get rid of this junk, we're going to head back to little old New York."

Felicia looked at him. He was a small man, scarcely as tall as she, but there was something about him that disturbed her. He had a strange, furtive look about his eyes and a way of staring when he talked.

They sat down at the table. Before Felicia had a chance to bow her head silently to ask the blessing, Herman Ewing shoved a bowl of steaming, warmed-over potatoes into her hand.

"Yes, sir!" he said. "We're mighty happy to have you girls here with us. But why did you come out here anyway?"

He shot the question bluntly, staring at first one and then the other.

"I'd think you'd want to be a little closer to the bright lights. There's nothing for girls your age way out here. No dances or anything."

Mrs. Ewing, who had been working at the stove, turned and was watching them closely.

"Yes," she said, "Herman and I have been wondering just why you came."

"It's as we told you," Joan said brightly. "We came out for a lark. And we thought we might poke around for some antiques at the same time."

Felicia felt her own checks pale.

"Who is this Miss Duncan you asked about?" Mrs. Ewing went on. "This woman you said was supposed to have written to us for a room for you?"

"She's the dean of women at the school we go to," Joan went on depreciatively. "She had to know where we were planning to go and what we were going to do every minute. So we asked her if she would write up here and get reservations for us. I suppose about the time we get ready to leave, you'll be hearing from her. That's the way she usually does things."

Felicia turned away to hide her confusion. Technically, perhaps, Joan wasn't lying. But for all practical purposes, she was deceiving the Ewings as surely as though she were lying to them.

Mrs. Ewing sought her gaze and held it forcibly.

There was a short, electric silence.

"Why are you here, Miss Cartright?" she asked. "You didn't come up here for a good time. Now did you?"

"To–to tell you the truth," Felicia answered slowly, "we came to see if we could find a certain antique sideboard."

"A sideboard!" Herman Ewing exclaimed, choking suddenly on his coffee.

The girls stared at Felicia, astonished.

"I–I–" Joan began uncertainly.

Mrs. Ewing, who had been standing at the stove, dropped the big spoon she was holding and took a step or two toward Felicia. Her face was a pasty, yellow mask.

"Did you say that you came up here looking for a sideboard?" she demanded.

CHAPTER 3

THE SEARCH PERMITTED

C larissa Ewing stepped closer to the girls, staring angrily at them. Her mouth was set in a firm line and her dark eyes were flashing. Her arms stiffened at her side.

"What was that about a sideboard?" she demanded again.

By this time Joan managed to smile.

"Felicia's aunt was very interested in sideboards," she said offhandedly. "And Felicia told her that we'd try to find her another one. That's what she meant about a sideboard."

Herman Ewing got up and poured another round of coffee. His bony hand was trembling, and his lips quivered slightly.

"Is that right?" Clarissa persisted, still eying Felicia.

"I–I am interested in antiques, that's true," she went on at last. "I've been interested in them ever since I've been in high school, I guess. My aunt runs an antique shop back home."

Joan took a deep breath and Gretchen relaxed a little.

"But," Felicia continued doggedly, "that isn't the reason that we're interested in the sideboard. You see, we attend Wellington School for Girls, the one Miss Grainger used to attend. She was supposed to have left an antique sideboard to the school, but nobody has been able to find it."

"See!" Herman Ewing said. "What did I tell you, Clarissa? Like I said, they'll just cause trouble. We should never have let them in."

"Herman!" Clarissa warned, her eyes scolding him.

The clock began to strike, ushering in a strange, unnatural silence. For the moment nobody moved or spoke. Mrs. Ewing was still glaring at her husband, anger lighting fires in her eyes. Then she turned to Felicia.

"You mustn't mind Herman," she said, trying desperately to smile. "He's been working so hard with everything that he's all upset."

"Clarissa's right," he broke in. "I didn't mean anything by what I said. We're right glad to have you girls."

"To tell you the truth," Clarissa continued, "we knew that you weren't just after antiques. We knew that three girls like you wouldn't be out here unless you were after something special and had a good idea where to look for it."

She sat down at the table across from them.

"But you should have told us. There isn't any call for you to keep your purpose here a secret. Goodness me, we'd be only too glad if you would find that sideboard, wouldn't we, Herman?"

He sipped his coffee without answering her.

"Wouldn't we, Herman?" she repeated. Her voice was soft, but delicately laced with acid.

"Oh, yes!" he blurted out, putting down his cup. "We'd be right happy if you would find it. The lawyer and a couple of guys from town were out here turning everything topsy-turvy, and a man from the school combed the place for three or four days. But he didn't find anything either."

"Besides, we've gone over everything ourselves," Clarissa added. "I know that sideboard would have been found long ago if it existed."

"So it isn't the idea that you might find it that bothers us," Herman went on. "It's just the nuisance of having you tear everything upside down."

"Now, Herman," his wife said with forced gentleness, "you could be a little more considerate. We don't mind having the girls here. They won't be much bother, and I'm sure they'll feel better if they have a chance to look around the place themselves."

"Thank you!" Felicia said.

"You're welcome to go anywhere you wish,"

Clarissa said, still smiling woodenly. "Into any of the rooms and in the attic and haymow. We want you to look around just as though you owned the place. We want you to be completely satisfied that we don't have the sideboard."

Her voice was pleasant enough, and there was a smile on her lips, but her eyes were dark and foreboding. Her hands were clenched tightly at her side, the cords showing livid and blue.

But for all the smiles and gestures of friendliness, the evening had gone suddenly sour. The girls sat there, talking little if at all. As soon as they finished eating, they went back to their room over the implement shed. Joan turned to Felicia.

"Did you see the looks on their faces?" she asked. "They'd like to help us find that sideboard all right!" Her lips curled sarcastically about the words. "What they'd really like to do is feed us strychnine."

Gretchen shuddered.

"Don't talk that way, Joan," she said. "The Ewings give me the cold chills anyway. They didn't take their eyes off us all the while we were in the house! And did you notice the way Herman looked at us when Felicia told him we were up here looking for that sideboard Miss Grainger left to Wellington?"

"Even though Miss Duncan and the people back at school don't believe that sideboard ever existed, Herman and Clarissa Ewing do," Felicia observed.

"They certainly do," Joan replied. "You could see

that by the looks on their faces. But why did you have to tell them why we were here, Felicia? Now we are in for plenty of trouble."

"They asked me," Felicia answered hesitantly.

"They asked me too," Joan told her. "Why didn't you stick with the story that I told them? Now they know why we're here. We aren't going to be able to make a single move without having one or the other of them peeking over our shoulders."

"You just about ruined everything," Gretchen put in.

"I–I couldn't lie to them," Felicia said, feeling the color come up into her cheeks. For a moment she looked away, but both Joan and Gretchen were watching her. She swallowed hard and got to her feet.

"I've never known that to bother you very much before," Joan said tartly. "I seem to remember some nights at school when you lied the same way the rest of us did in order to get out on a restricted evening."

"I know that," Felicia answered. "I'm certainly not proud of it, but I have to admit that it's true."

Gretchen started to speak, but there was something about Felicia's manner that stopped her.

"I've been wanting to tell you this for a long time," she went on. "But somehow, it's been awfully hard for me. You both mentioned that I act differently now than I did when I left last June."

Joan nodded. "But what's that got to do with it?"

"Everything. You see, I am different now." She

took a deep breath and, getting to her feet, grasped the back of the chair for support. "This summer I did what you were ridiculing Miss Grainger for advocating, Joan. I–I became a Christian."

There was a long, tense silence.

"What?" Joan echoed, her eyes widening.

"I don't blame you for being surprised," Felicia went on, gaining courage as she spoke. "But I trusted the Lord Jesus as my personal Savior. That's why I couldn't lie to the Ewings."

"You?" Joan asked in disbelief. "'Dancing Feet' Cartright, a Christian? Why, I just can't believe it."

Felicia knew that her cheeks were scarlet. It was all that she could do to keep looking at her roommates. She wanted to turn and flee. But she could not stop now.

"I can hardly believe it myself," she went on, "but they have been the happiest days of my life. You have no idea what a joy it is to be a Christian and to put your trust in the Lord Jesus for everything."

Gretchen smiled condescendingly.

"I think you would have been the last one I would have expected to take a step like that, Felicia," she said. "I always thought you were too practical, too – shall we say – intelligent to be taken in by that sort of thing."

Felicia swallowed hard. She should keep talking with Gretchen about the Lord Jesus. She ought to tell her more about Him, of the joy that comes from serving Him, of the happiness that a Christian can have in knowing that the sin in her life has been forgiven. But try as she would, she could not speak.

For a long while after they went to bed that night, Felicia lay awake looking up into the darkness. If only she could find the words to tell them how wonderful it was to know the Lord.

The next morning after breakfast, Mrs. Ewing took the girls into the living room of the big, old-fashioned house.

"Herman and I talked it over last night," she said. "We decided that it would be better for you to start here and go through the house systematically. You may go anywhere you wish and open any doors you wish. We want you to be completely satisfied that the sideboard isn't here." She stopped for a moment. "And who knows," she went on, "perhaps you will be able to do what nobody else has been able to do and find the sideboard."

"Thank you," Felicia said, looking around. "We'll try not to cause you any trouble."

"That's quite all right."

The young Christian girl was fascinated by the great beamed ceiling and the old-fashioned fireplace with the tile hearth and the period furniture placed so fittingly about the room that she scarcely heard what Mrs. Ewing had said.

"If you find any doors that are locked or anything that you need help with," Clarissa continued curtly, "feel free to call on us. When you go back to Wellington, we don't want either you or the school authorities to think that we obstructed you in any way."

Before the girls could answer, she turned and walked away, leaving them alone. They stood there a moment or two uncertainly, looking around.

"This place still gives me the creeps," Gretchen said, shivering. "I don't know why we ever came up here in the first place."

The house had been left exactly as Miss Grainger and her parents had had it fifty years before, except for the three rooms at the back where the Ewings lived. Those rooms had been wired with electricity, and a bath had been installed there and in the servants' quarters. But the rest of the house was just as it had always been.

The beautiful old lamps were still set on exquisite little tables. And the sofa and chairs, straight-backed with deep, velvet seats, looked as though they had come from a great museum, or the floor of an exclusive antique dealer. The rugs were thick and soft underfoot. Long, dark-hued drapes hung at the windows. Except for the dust, which lay like a shroud on everything, the rooms were like pieces of yesterday.

"I don't see how a beautiful place like this can give you the creeps," Felicia exclaimed as they stepped from one beautifully furnished room to another. "It's charming."

"Charming or not," Joan said laconically, "there are no sideboards lying around. That much is certain."

CHAPTER 4

A MYSTERIOUS NIGHT PICKUP

The girls went over the house carefully – from room to room, poking into closets and behind doors, and going up into the attic.

It was almost noon when they finished their exploration and went back to the kitchen where Mrs. Ewing was fixing lunch. She did not look up when they entered but continued to stir the gravy she was making.

"Well," she asked sharply, "did you find it?"

Joan shook her head. "No, we didn't," she answered.

Mrs. Ewing turned off the stove and poured the gravy into a large bowl.

"Did you look carefully?" she asked.

"We turned the place inside out," Joan answered, "but no sideboard. If the thing is in the house, it would have to be knocked down and stashed away in a drawer somewhere."

Clarissa brushed a few strands of hair from her haggard face. "I certainly hope this is the last group of people who come here to look for that sideboard," she said. "It seems as though every time we turn around, there's somebody else nosing into our things and looking at Herman and me as though we're a pair of criminals. It's getting to be quite an imposition."

That afternoon Felicia and her companions went through the barn and the implement shed. They, too, were exactly as the Graingers had left them. The ancient surrey, its black paint still gleaming beneath the dust, was standing in an unused portion of the shed. The fringe around the top was still in place, the tassels faded by age, and the iron tires were tight on the narrow wheels. Next to it was a little cutter with rusty runners, but the paint on it was still clean and new. And the long willow whip was still in the socket. In the back of the shed hung old axes, an ice saw that hadn't been used for years, and a host of tools which Felicia had never seen before and could only guess at their purpose.

Still she went poking around, moving boxes, and peering with eager excitement into the huge barrels and crates. Her hands were black, and there was a smudge of dirt across her forehead and on the bridge of her nose.

Joan sat down wearily, wiping her moist forehead with the back of her hand.

"There's everything under the sun in this place," she said, "except that sideboard."

"If Mr. Wharton couldn't find it when he was here," Gretchen said for the third time, "I don't see how we can expect to."

There was a little door to the back and off to one side of the implement shed.

"I wonder what's in here," Felicia asked aloud.

"Mr. Ewing uses it as a feed room," a voice said curtly behind her.

She turned to see Clarissa Ewing standing there.

The woman had come up so silently that none of the girls had heard her. For an instant she glared at Felicia, her hair streaking across her thin cheekbones and her mouth drawn down to a thin line.

"We are in it every day," she went on, almost belligerently. "If the sideboard were in there, we most assuredly would have seen it. But I'll get the key to it from my husband in the morning. We will want you to go through it before you leave."

"If you've been using it all the time, there's not much point in our examining it," Felicia told her. "You surely would have seen the sideboard had it been there."

"Yes," Clarissa said, smirking, "but you wouldn't know. We want you to see for yourselves."

Felicia got out her Bible that evening and read a chapter to herself. Both Gretchen and Joan watched in obvious amusement.

"If you're doing that for our benefit," Joan told her, laughing, "you're wasting your time. We're not going to be taken in just because you are."

Felicia flushed.

"Ever since I became a Christian, I've been reading my Bible regularly," she said.

"My," Gretchen answered, "you do have it bad, don't you?"

"I wouldn't call it that," Felicia countered.

The girls had been in bed for only an hour or so and had just dropped off to sleep when Felicia heard a noise outside.

She must not have been sleeping soundly, for at the first faint, rasping noise she opened her eyes. She didn't realize where she was for a moment and lay there pulling her senses together and driving the sleep away. She heard it again, an indistinct, muffled noise that was so soft she could scarcely believe that she had heard anything at all.

She raised up on one elbow, straining to hear. But the only sound in the big pitch-dark room was the rhythmic breathing of her companions.

And then she heard the sound again – a little louder and coming from directly below them.

"Gretchen!" she whispered tensely, reaching across to the single bed where her friend was sleeping and touching her. "Joan! Wake up!"

Gretchen stirred sleepily.

"Wake up!" she whispered again, shaking her.

"There's somebody down in the implement shed! Wake up!"

Gretchen sat bolt upright, rubbing the sleep from her eyes with her fists.

"What's the matter?" she mumbled. "What's wrong?"

By this time, Joan was groaning sleepily. She turned over and sat up, only half awake.

"Joan," Felicia said again, "wake up!"

"What's the matter?" Gretchen asked, getting to her feet.

"Did you hear that?"

Gretchen had moved close to Felicia. She put her hand on the girl's shoulder, her long, slender fingers digging into the flesh.

"Did–did you hear what I did?" Felicia asked again.

"There–there's somebody down there," Gretchen said numbly. "They're moving something down below us!"

There were strange sounds coming from the implement shed just below them – a dull scraping noise of heavy objects being scooted along the cement floor.

"Somebody is down there!" Joan exclaimed, suddenly realizing why Felicia had awakened her. "What are they doing?"

All three of them had been so startled that they had frozen where they were, not daring to move.

Then there was the muffled sound of a motor starting just outside. Gretchen sprang to the window.

"They're leaving!" she cried.

Gretchen reached the window and jerked back the shade, but she was too late. She was just in time to see an ancient jeep pickup pull slowly away.

"They must have taken something out of the implement shed," Felicia said weakly. "I thought I could hear them down there, but I couldn't get you two awake."

"We'd better get the Ewings," Joan said. "Somebody must have stolen something."

"There was something on the back of that truck," Gretchen whispered excitedly. "I saw it."

"We'd better go down and see Mr. Ewing," Felicia repeated. "He'll want to get the authorities right away."

Hurriedly the three girls slipped into their robes. Joan took a flashlight from the dresser and started toward the door. The other two followed her. The flashlight stabbed a faint, yellow hole in the almost impenetrable darkness that squeezed about them like a shroud. They followed it down the stairs and stopped for a moment, looking in the big door to the implement shed, sweeping the contents with the light.

Whoever had been in the implement shed had known exactly what to look for. Boxes and barrels had been cast hurriedly aside. The girls could see, almost at a glance, that nothing had been taken from them.

"What do you suppose they were after?" Joan asked.

There was a short, tense silence.

"Look!" Felicia gasped. "The door to the feed room is open!"

Gretchen reached out and took hold of Joan's arm. "Something heavy has been taken out of there too," she declared softly, pointing with a trembling finger toward the floor. "Look at those marks in the dust."

Felicia felt suddenly weak.

"Mrs. Ewing told us that there was nothing in there except feed."

"You'll find out one of these days that people don't always tell you the truth," Joan said. "And I can tell you this much, we'd be a lot better off if you hadn't been too religious to lie a little. Come on."

They stepped slowly, almost reluctantly, toward the little room. The light revealed a large, rectangular square in the dust on the feed room floor.

"Something big has been in here, all right," Joan said. "Just look at that big place where it was."

"That could have been a piece of furniture too," Felicia added excitedly. "But why would they have put it out here in the feed room?"

"Unless it was that sideboard we've been looking for," Gretchen observed. "You know, we roamed all over the house, poking into every nook and cranny, and there was only one locked door in the place. This feed room is the only spot we haven't looked in."

"I'd never thought of that," Joan said.

They huddled together in the darkness, talking in low whispers.

"And do you remember how strangely Mr. Ewing acted last night when his wife said she wanted him to show us the feed room this morning?" Joan Bailey went on. "As soon as he finished eating, he excused himself and went outside. We didn't see any more of him either."

"And now we hear strange noises in the middle of the night," Felicia whispered, "and see a jeep pickup drive away."

"That sideboard could have sat right there in the dust."

"But if it belongs to the school," Joan asked, "why would they try to hide it from us? Just as soon as the sideboard goes on the market the school could claim it."

"Don't you remember?" Gretchen said. "Wellington has to claim that sideboard within six months, or it belongs to Clarissa and Herman Ewing."

The girls stood there, staring at one another in the semidarkness.

"Nobody would have dared to drive up to the house this way and break open the feed room with us upstairs and the Ewings in this corner of the house," Felicia said thoughtfully. "Besides, whoever broke in here had the key to the feed room and knew where to find what they were after. I don't think anything else was taken."

"It certainly doesn't look like it," Gretchen observed.

"There are only two people who knew what was in the feed room and had access to the key."

"Clarissa and Herman Ewing!" Joan exclaimed. "We might have known it!"

"We'd better be getting back to our room," Felicia whispered hoarsely. "There's no telling when they'll come back or what they'd do if they found out that we discovered anything about this little affair tonight."

"Just a minute," Joan said as the other two started toward the door. "I'm going to take a quick look around while we've got the chance."

She probed the far corners of the little feed room with the flashlight.

"Hurry, Joan!" Gretchen said nervously. "They've been gone quite a while. They're liable to be back any minute."

She had stopped halfway to the door and was looking around nervously.

"I'll be with you in a jiffy," Joan said. And then the flashlight beam revealed a white square of heavy paper. "What's this?" she said, picking it up.

"Hurry up, Joan!" Felicia said.

But the dark-haired girl was staring intently at the piece of paper she held in her hand.

"Why, it's a picture!" she said.

Felicia gasped when she saw it.

"That was taken at the museum in Boston!" she exclaimed.

"But why?"

"I don't know why," she replied, "but I'd know it anywhere. That's a closeup of the old Parker sideboard in the new Boston museum."

Gretchen's hands were trembling as she reached for the picture.

"But why would it be here?" she asked. "What would they want with a picture of this sideboard? Especially if they had the one Miss Grainger had left to the school?"

"Maybe they got this picture of the Parker sideboard in Boston to check with the one they found here to see if it was genuine."

Felicia took the picture and turned it over. "Just look at the date this was developed," she said. "Just a week after the notice the school got that Miss Grainger had willed the sideboard to them."

"Do you suppose that means anything?" Joan asked impatiently.

Gretchen shook her head.

"It could mean a great deal," she whispered.

CHAPTER 5

FOLLOWING THE JEEP'S TRAIL

The girls were still standing in the room when they saw a light come slowly down the county road and turn in the lane.

"Come on!" Joan cried, running toward the stairs. "Here they come! We can't let them catch us here now!"

Gretchen and Felicia turned and fled, stumbling over the boxes in their haste.

"Hurry!" Gretchen stammered. "They'll be here any minute!"

They scrambled upstairs in the darkness. As they rushed into their room they saw the lights, through the window, jouncing down the rough lane toward the house.

"That was close!" Gretchen panted, standing tensely beside the window and staring out at the side of the shade. "They almost caught us!"

"I didn't realize that we had stayed downstairs so long," Felicia gasped.

"I tried to tell you both," Joan said matter-of-factly. "But we know this much, at least. They had something in that feed room that they didn't want us to see."

"It must be that sideboard," Felicia said determinedly. "It almost has to be."

"If it were," Gretchen put in, "it's gone now, and we'll probably never find it again."

"Wherever they went," Joan added, "they couldn't have taken it too far. They weren't gone long enough."

They lay in bed for a long while, talking now and then, or closing their eyes and feigning sleep. Finally, they dozed off, and it was not until they heard Herman Ewing open the shed door directly below them that they awakened.

"Now, whatever you do, when you get down there, Felicia," Joan ordered, "don't spill the beans about what we heard last night. If they ever find out that we know they took something out of that feed room, we're sunk. We had just as well go back to Wellington and forget all about this."

Felicia nodded.

"My, but you girls slept soundly last night," Mrs. Ewing said when they finally came down to breakfast. "I was about ready to put the dishes away and make you wait until lunch time to eat."

Felicia looked at her watch. "I guess that would

have been all right," she said. "It wouldn't have been such a long wait at that."

"How did you sleep last night?" Clarissa Ewing persisted.

Felicia looked quickly over at Joan and Gretchen. Nobody spoke.

"To tell you the truth," Clarissa went on, "I've been a little worried about those beds. The mattresses aren't quite as good as they could be."

All the while she spoke her gaze darted from one girl to the next, probing shamelessly.

"If you think those beds are hard," Joan laughed, "you ought to see the ones we sleep on at school. I think they were made at least a hundred years before these beds you've got."

Clarissa Ewing sighed with evident relief.

"Well, you'd better sit up and eat now. Herman wants to show you the feed room before he goes to work. He's been waiting for you for the last hour."

"Oh," Gretchen said quickly, "it won't be necessary to show us into that room now. We've already–"

"You already *what?*" Mrs. Ewing demanded suspiciously.

"Oh, I think we ought to look in there by all means," Joan said, kicking her friend, and not too gently, under the table. "You know that was the room that was locked when we went through the implement shed yesterday afternoon, Gretchen."

Felicia looked down at her plate, expecting Clarissa

to continue her probing, but Herman came in just then whirling a ring of keys on his index finger.

"Well," he said, laughing, "are you amateur sleuths ready to go out and start looking for clues? I'm about ready to go to work."

The girls smiled uneasily.

They finished eating as quickly as possible and went to the feed room with Herman. Clarissa had said nothing about going along, but by the time they reached the implement shed she was close behind them.

"Now, we'll see what we've got in here," Herman said with a flourish.

Felicia started when he opened the door. The room had been empty the night before, except for the dust on the floor and a box in one corner. Now it was piled high with tools and feed that had been thrown about with studied carelessness, as though it had been the accumulation of months of use. The floor had been swept and the broom put away.

"Well, I–," she began, stopping as she caught herself.

"Never did have all that junk out of the back of the feed room," Herman lied. "If you want me to, I'll get it out so you can see what's back there. But I know there isn't space enough for your precious sideboard."

For a long while the girls did not speak. They stood looking around the room.

Clarissa stepped forward and began to peer intently at the floor.

"What are you looking for, Clarissa?" Herman asked.

"Oh, nothing." She straightened and turned back toward the door. "I misplaced a little picture the other day, and I've been looking everywhere for it. I thought perhaps it was out here."

"What kind of a picture?"

A faint flush came into the woman's cheeks. "It was just a picture," she retorted firmly. "It isn't anything that would interest you at all."

Herman eyed her quizzically for an instant, then turned to Felicia.

"Well," he asked, his voice rising, "are you satisfied now that the sideboard isn't here?"

"Oh, yes!" she answered. "Thank you!"

He grunted unintelligibly. "I think I'll be getting to work then." He stepped back and carefully locked the feed room.

As soon as Herman and Clarissa were gone, Felicia took Joan by the arm.

"Come on," she said, "let's pretend to keep on looking in the barn."

"There's something out here that I'd like to see about first," Joan countered. "Did you notice that those jeep tracks were just as plain as could be right up to the implement shed door?"

Gretchen's face lit up. "Maybe we can follow them and find out where Herman took the sideboard."

Felicia looked apprehensively up toward the house.

"We can't stand here talking. They'll get suspicious. Let's act as though we're giving up on the sideboard and going for a walk. They don't know that we saw them last night."

"That's right," Joan broke in. "If we act casual enough, they'll think we've decided the sideboard isn't anywhere around and that we're giving up the search."

Nevertheless, as they sauntered up the lane, Clarissa came to the door. "Are you going to be gone long?" she asked.

"We ought to be back in time for lunch," Felicia replied.

"The country is so beautiful here that we just wanted to look around a little before we go back to school," Joan added.

The girls walked almost to the end of the lane before anybody spoke.

"Why did you tell her that?" Felicia asked Joan gently. "She didn't ask where we were going. There wasn't any need to lie to her."

The other girl laughed. "I'm not bothered about that the way you are," she said. "You remember, I'm one of those who still needs saving."

Felicia looked away, her eyes smarting.

"You don't suppose the Ewings will try to follow us this morning, do you?" Gretchen asked a few moments later as they turned south along the county road, looking intently at the roadbed for the telltale tracks of the old jeep.

"It doesn't make any difference whether they do or not," Joan said easily. "We're just out for a walk, enjoying the beautiful scenery. We like to hike, you know." She paused and looked obliquely at the Christian girl who was walking beside her. "Of course, if Felicia had gotten a chance to talk to them, she could have told them where we were going and what we intended to do. You know, she's gotten so good all of a sudden."

Felicia squirmed under the sarcasm, but Gretchen acted as though she hadn't even heard.

"I don't know how you feel about it," she said, lowering her voice, "but there's something very strange going on here. I don't like it at all."

Felicia picked up the track in the soft dirt at the side of the road and began to follow it. Gretchen and Joan caught up with her.

"I just wonder," she said softly, pausing to look apprehensively into the deep forest on either side of the narrow trail. "Do you suppose they do have that sideboard hidden out here somewhere?"

"It could be," Joan said. "After Mr. Wharton came and made his search for the school, they could have thought the coast was clear. Then when we showed up, they had to do something."

"After all," Gretchen put in, "they only have to keep it hidden from us for a few more days. The six months which Miss Grainger allotted to the school to claim the sideboard are almost up."

The smile left Joan's face. "They'll do anything to keep us from finding it," she said.

"But if we do find it and the proof that it is a genuine Parker," Felicia countered, "they won't be able to keep us from taking it. All we've got to do is to get in touch with the authorities at school. They'll do the rest."

"And convince them that we know what we're talking about," Joan answered. "Miss Duncan thinks we're a little nuts for coming up here in the first place."

They were still standing there talking when Gretchen grasped Felicia by the arm. Her face was white, and her fingers were trembling.

"There–there's somebody in those bushes!" she whispered hoarsely.

Felicia felt her mouth go dry. The strength drained from her body. For an instant, she went limp, incapable of moving.

Joan Bailey's face was ashen and her forehead moist with perspiration.

"I caught a glimpse of him!" Gretchen repeated, her voice quavering. "He's squatting down behind those bushes, staring at us!"

"*What are we going to do?*"

CHAPTER 6

THE CABIN IN THE WOODS

I can still see his eyes!" Gretchen whispered. "He's staring at us!"

There was a rustle in the brush. The girls stiffened.

"He's coming out!" Gretchen shrilled.

With that, their fear found legs. They whirled and began to run as fast as they could up the narrow, twisting road. Whoever it was might take after them, Felicia told herself as they ran. He would want to stop them before they got back to the Grainger house. He would–

But she dared not think about that now. She ran until her legs throbbed and her lungs were screaming for air. She ran until she could run no more. Felicia took a quick look back, but there was no sign of anyone on the road behind them.

"I–I don't think anyone is following us," she panted, slowing down. The other girls did the same.

"Do you suppose he's following along after us in the brush?" Gretchen gasped, glancing wildly around.

"I don't think so," Joan said, sinking to the ground. "He couldn't scramble through the trees fast enough to keep up with us."

"Do you remember how Clarissa Ewing eyed us as we left?" Felicia asked. "She might have guessed what we were doing, and Herman could have followed us to see where we went and what we did."

"I don't think it was Herman," Gretchen said doubtfully. "Those eyes were hollow and sunken and stared right through me." A spasm of fear shook her. "I can still see them! And that scraggly white beard."

"You were probably imagining things," Joan said, laughing a little.

"I might have been imagining the beard," Gretchen told her, "but I didn't imagine those eyes. I can still see them."

When the girls had rested for a few minutes, they got up and walked in silence toward the house.

"Now listen," Joan finally said, "when we go into that house, we've got to act as though nothing happened. We've just been out for a nice little walk. We haven't seen or heard anything. Do you understand?"

"As long as we don't have to lie about it," was Felicia's answer.

"You've certainly turned Puritan all of a sudden," Joan said. "You'd better let Gretchen and me do the talking. You'll just get us into trouble with this Christian honesty of yours."

They hadn't been gone from the big, old house too long, and lunch wasn't ready when they got back. But as they went into the kitchen, both Herman and Clarissa were sitting at the table, their heads bent close together.

They jumped as the girls came in.

"Don't you have any better manners than to enter a house without knocking?" Clarissa demanded, her sharp features clouding. "I thought they taught you how to act at that school you attend."

"I – that is, we're sorry," Felicia stammered. They had been entering the house without knocking ever since they first came. In fact, Herman Ewing had told them to treat the place as they would their own home. Clarissa had agreed.

"We–we were just sitting here looking at the Bible," Herman said, fumbling for words. "It's a mighty good Book to take a look at once in a while."

Gretchen and Joan and Felicia were all staring at the well-worn Bible that lay open on the table between Herman and Clarissa.

"That's quite all right," Joan said, smirking as she looked at Felicia. "And if you've got any questions you'd like to ask, just come to Felicia. She's made herself quite the expert on it the past few months."

"You have?" Herman echoed, turning toward

her. "Then maybe you can tell me a couple of things about it."

"Oh, she'd be glad to," Joan Bailey broke in. "She's always trying to talk to us about it. She's a regular little missionary."

"What's got me puzzled is–"

"Herman," Clarissa broke in sharply, "I need another load of wood for the cook stove in case it turns cold."

"But I just filled the wood box this morning," he protested. "And besides, you've been cooking on that gas stove for the past two weeks."

"Bring in another load of wood," Clarissa snapped, "and don't be talking so much."

The girls ate lunch and went back to their room.

"Well," Joan said as soon as they were alone together, "we know now that it wasn't Clarissa and Herman who were spying on us back in the woods. Herman wouldn't have had time enough to have gotten back to the house before we did."

"I suppose the next thing you'll both be trying to tell me is that I didn't see anybody back there on the road," Gretchen said. "But I know I did. I saw him just as plainly as I can see either of you. And, whoever he was, he wanted to keep himself hidden."

"I'm certainly glad that he didn't try to come after us," Felicia told her, "whoever he was."

"By the way," Joan said after a moment or two, "did you notice what the Ewings were reading when we went into the house, Felicia? I see that you and Herman and Clarissa have quite a bit in common."

Gretchen smiled a little, condescendingly. The corners of her mouth lifted, and she tossed her head, as though to show how superior she was for not having fallen for that "Christian business," as she called it.

"That's right, Felicia!" she added. "And come to think of it, it's very easy to see why the Ewings are interested in the Bible. Just look at the pinched little lives they're living. That, actually, is the sort of people that Christianity appeals to. They can't get anything worthwhile out of life, so they try to compensate for it by adopting a faith that gives them all the things they don't have."

Felicia winced.

"The Christians that I've known aren't like that," she said defensively. "It takes the best that any of us have to live the way Christ wants us to live. And, as far as compensating for unhappiness, how about those people who flit from one party to another? Some of them jump from one wife or husband to another, and often end up as alcoholics because they can't face life. Wouldn't you say that they're afraid to face life as it is? And you surely couldn't call them Christian."

Gretchen was silent.

Joan looked at Felicia appraisingly.

"You're really serious about this, aren't you?" she asked. There was admiration in her voice. "I honestly thought that you were stringing us a line when you first mentioned it. That you were having a little fun by pretending to be like old Miss Grainger."

"No," Felicia answered, "I've never been more serious in my life. I'm not giving you a line when I tell you how much it means to me to know Christ as my Savior. It's made a complete change in my life. I–I don't know whether I can find the words to explain it or not, but I've confessed my sins and have put my trust in Christ for salvation. I'm not the old Felicia Cartright that you used to know."

Joan sat up, and for a long minute eyed her quizzically.

"I do have to admit," she said, "that I've noticed a change in you." She spoke almost wistfully. "It must be comforting to have a faith like that."

"It is," Felicia answered. "It's the happiest, most comforting life anyone could possibly live."

"Well," Gretchen broke in hurriedly, "thinking about that sideboard isn't so comforting. We've only got a few days to find it and uncover the proof that it's a genuine Parker, or the school is going to lose its claim to it."

Joan wanted to go back into the woods to discover where the jeep had gone, but the other two decided against it.

"We'd better act as though we aren't interested," Gretchen said.

"Besides," Joan countered, "you might see the man with those haunting eyes again."

Gretchen turned to face her. "I just wish you'd see him," she retorted. "I wish you'd see him just once!"

While the other girls slept, Felicia wrote a letter to her mother, then began to read her Bible. She was still reading when Joan awakened.

"You know, I was just thinking something, Joan," she said as soon as her friend sat up. "Did it strike you as strange that the Ewings would be reading the Bible when we came in this morning? They're definitely not the type to be so interested in the Scriptures."

"I was thinking the same thing myself," Joan answered. "And they were so disturbed when we caught them at it. They acted as though it had something to do with that sideboard, or at least that was the way it seemed to me."

"Herman did act awfully strange," Gretchen added. It was the first the other two knew that she was awake. "And so did Clarissa. She sent him out after an armload of wood to shut him up."

It was after dinner that evening, and the girls were about ready for bed when Gretchen went to the window and stood for a moment or two with the shade up, looking out into the darkness.

"Joan," she said, "didn't the Ewings say the front part of the house was not wired for electricity?"

"That's right," she said from her place beside the desk where she was squinting to read by the flickering yellow light of the kerosene lamp.

"Blow out that light and come here."

She opened the window when Joan had blown out the lamp and, loosening the screen, she thrust her head out to look along the side of the darkened house.

"What do you see?" Joan asked.

"I thought I saw a light shining on the ground at the front of the house," Gretchen replied after a moment or two. "But I could have been mistaken."

They watched in silence for a minute or two.

"I can see it now," Joan said. "Look over there."

Even as they watched, it went out again, leaving the house in darkness.

"Somebody's over in the front part of the house," Gretchen whispered tensely. "They've got a flashlight and are going from room to room."

"That could only be Herman and Clarissa," Felicia observed. "Nobody else would dare to go into the house when they were in there sleeping."

"Why do you suppose they're going around like that?" Joan asked. "If they moved the sideboard the other night, why would they still be hunting around in the house? Do you suppose we were mistaken about that affair the other night? Could that sideboard still be in the house?"

"That's one of the things that we'll have to find out," answered Felicia.

The following morning the girls got up and ate an early breakfast. And, as quickly as possible, they went out along the road.

"Do you think you'll be back for lunch?" Clarissa

asked, probing again with those dark, searching eyes of hers.

"We were going for a walk," Joan said. "It would be nice if you could fix us a little lunch. We aren't sure just when we'll be back."

"Well," Clarissa said reluctantly, "I suppose I could fix you something to eat if you're determined to go. But Herman and I don't approve of your tramping around in the forest that way. You're apt to get lost and cause us all a sight of trouble."

"Oh, we're not going back into the woods far enough to get lost," Joan said. "But we aren't sure whether we'd be back in time for lunch or not. That's why we thought we'd like to take some sandwiches along."

Clarissa fixed them something to eat, grumbling as she did, and packed it in a cardboard box.

"Do you suppose that we dare go back in the woods to the place where that jeep turned off?" Gretchen asked as they walked along the lane away from the house.

"We've got to," Felicia said. "That's the only chance we'll have to find out where that sideboard is."

"We'd better head up the road, though," Joan suggested, "and make Clarissa and Herman think we're headed toward the highway. When we get out of sight, we can go into the forest and double back."

"That sounds like a good idea," Gretchen said. "I certainly don't want them to follow us too."

"You'd better stop that kind of talk," Joan Bailey

told her, "or you'll have both Felicia and me heading back to the house to hide our heads under our pillows."

It took them half an hour longer, but when they got to the lane and stopped momentarily, they saw that Clarissa was standing in the back door watching them.

"Don't look now," Felicia cautioned, "but we're getting the once-over."

With a great show of carelessness, the girls headed north toward the main highway. As they did so Clarissa went back into the house.

"She thinks we're going in a safe direction," Joan said softly. "I don't think they can see us from here, do you? Wouldn't it be safe to head back now?"

"I believe we'd better go around this next bend," Gretchen said cautiously. "Clarissa can't see us from here, but we don't know for sure where Herman is."

"He's out in the woods," Joan scoffed. "We don't have to worry about him."

"Unless he headed over toward the place where they drove the jeep the other night."

"You think of the pleasantest things!"

They stayed off the road until they had backtracked almost half a mile. Then they went out onto the narrow county road and walked to the place where the jeep had turned off into the woods. By this time the tracks were gone, and they had to guess about the logging road where the jeep had turned. The day before they had seen the tracks plainly. Now they were gone.

"Do you suppose this is the right road?" Joan asked when they came to a narrow, twisting, grass-covered trail that wandered off into the forest.

Gretchen looked about fearfully. "Yes," she said, shuddering. "This is it all right. There's the place where the man was hiding!"

"Is he still there?" Joan asked with a smile.

"Quick!" Felicia said suddenly. "Into the brush! There's someone coming!"

Frantically the three girls hurried into the brush and flung themselves to the ground. They were just in time. The jeep went slowly by. At the place where the logging road entered the woods it stopped for almost a minute. Felicia and her companions pressed closer to the ground, hardly daring to breathe. Then the jeep started again, slowly, and went on down the county road.

"That was Herman!" Gretchen whispered.

"Clarissa must have been suspicious," Joan said, "even though we headed the other direction. She sent Herman out to check on us to be sure we didn't come over this way."

"Then there must be something out here that they don't want us to see."

"At any rate we fooled him," Joan said, getting to her feet. "He stopped here and looked up the road.

He must have figured that we went the other direction, or he'd have driven in to check."

"We'd better hurry," Gretchen put in nervously. "He'll probably just drive down to the next crossroad to turn around and come back. We don't want him to catch us out here."

They hurried down the logging trail without talking. They listened intently as they walked for the dreadful sound of the jeep in case Herman should decide to drive down the trail. But fifteen minutes passed, and then twenty, and there was no sign of him.

"I guess we gave him the slip," Joan said, sighing. "Now if we can just find out why he and Clarissa drove in here the other night, we'll be on the way to unraveling this mystery."

They had walked along the trail for half a mile or so, when at last they came to a small pond, with a dilapidated old cabin standing beside it.

"Look!" Joan cried excitedly, as she spied the building through the trees.

"I thought this was an old logging road," Felicia said. "I didn't have any idea there was a cabin back here."

"An old cabin back in the woods this way would be an ideal place to hide that sideboard," Gretchen said. "Probably nobody's been back in here for years and years."

Their hearts began to pound more excitedly as they neared the cabin. It was a small one-room building with a single, homemade door and two windows. The glass had been broken out of the lower pane that was closest to the door, and somebody had covered the opening with a piece of wood.

"You don't mean to tell me that people used to live in places like this?" Gretchen asked incredulously. "Right out here in the forest?"

Neither of the other girls answered her. Felicia moaned as she moved toward the door.

"Oh, it's locked!" she exclaimed in despair.

"And with a new padlock too!"

Joan examined it carefully. "Why would anybody put a new latch and padlock on a cabin like this?" she asked. "Surely it isn't worth that much!"

Felicia walked over to the window and peered inside. It was dark, but she could make out the dim outline of a huge object in the opposite corner.

"There's something over there in that corner," she whispered. "It's big enough to be the sideboard, and it's got a blanket wrapped around it."

"Here," Joan said, trying to push her aside, "let me see."

"It does look like it's made of walnut," Gretchen observed, peering over their shoulders. "See that one leg where the blanket doesn't cover it all."

"That's right," Felicia said excitedly. "And that's just the way the leg of the Parker sideboard would look. See how it's made, so full and massive and right down to the floor."

"Then the Ewings did know where that sideboard was after all!"

The three girls were crowded around the window, still staring into the dingy little cabin. There was a footstep behind them, but none of them heard it. It came so quietly, and then a voice spoke.

"Are you girls looking for something?" a quavering voice demanded.

Felicia, Joan, and Gretchen froze instantly! A spasm of fear chilled the blood in their veins!

CHAPTER 7

THE ELDERLY STRANGER

The girls stood there at the window, their bodies stiffening! Cold beads of sweat stood out on their foreheads!

"What are ye doing here?" the voice croaked again.

It was a weak, uncertain voice, but there was strength in it – strength that was frightening.

Felicia turned slowly, catching her breath. She was staring into the watery blue eyes of a wizened, bent old man who was scarcely as tall as she as he leaned forward on his cane. His heavily bearded face was wrinkled and burned dark by countless days in the sun, and his gnarled, bony hands were clasped tightly around the head of the heavy cane that was twisted as he was. His gaze did not leave their faces.

"I've seen ye snooping around these parts," he went on. "I seen ye yesterday. Who be ye? And what do ye want around here? We don't hanker much for folks that comes a-snoopin'."

It was Joan Bailey who spoke first.

"But we weren't snooping," she protested. "We just came upon this darling little cabin and thought that we'd like to see what was inside. We didn't mean any harm."

"What were ye doing here yesterday?" he asked. "And why did ye come back today?"

"We're staying at the Ewings," Joan explained, ignoring his questions.

"Hmph!" he grunted disgustedly. "Them!"

He spoke as though the very name was a swear word.

"Actually, though," Felicia went on, "we're from Wellington College in Connecticut. We're taking our holiday up here."

The old man's eyes narrowed for an instant and then brightened. He pursed his lips.

"Wellington?" he echoed. "That's a school for girls, ain't it? That's the school Miss Martha went to. Did you know Miss Martha?"

"Do you mean Martha Grainger?" Felicia asked. "Yes, she went to school there a long while ago."

He nodded vigorously.

"I knowed that was it. I knowed it as soon as I heard it. The fact is, I figured maybe that's where ye was from all along."

"But what made you think that?" Joan demanded.

He pointed his finger at her and shook it disapprovingly.

"Now hold on there a minute, young lady," he said, "I'll tell ye when I get good and ready. Don't you get so plumb uppity with me." He settled back down on his cane, leaning forward heavily.

"But what about Miss Grainger?" Gretchen asked.

"I used to look after things for Miss Martha and her pa," he said. "For nigh onto forty years I took care of everything for them. Lived right there in the house with them. Until she died and them Ewings came along!"

"That's right," Joan said. "I remember now. You were mentioned in the will. You're Jasper Denton."

"That's right, young lady," he said. "Not that it made no difference. I didn't need their money. I can take care of myself." He lowered his voice. "But she give me something for ye. Said it was very important, and I should watch out and give it to the folks from the college when they come along. I've been waiting and watching every day. I've been 'spectin' ye."

"What is it?" Joan asked excitedly. "Was it a piece of paper or some furniture?"

She questioned him hopefully, but he rambled on, as though he did not even hear her.

"I don't think she trusted them Ewings much," he said, turning his head and spitting contemptuously. "And I know that I don't! They've been snooping around my place. I've been fixin' to get out my shotgun and run 'em off if it keeps up. They got no business trespassing that way."

For a moment or two the girls stared at one another bewilderedly. First the Ewings made a midnight trip with their jeep pickup. Then they were walking about the big house with a flashlight in the middle of the night. Now they learned that they had been nosing around Jasper Denton's. It didn't add up. It didn't add up at all.

"I've got to be sure that you're who ye say ye are," he continued. "Else I won't tell you nothing about it, let alone give it to ye."

Felicia thought for a moment.

"Did you ever see the ring Miss Grainger wore?" she asked, holding out her hand. "Didn't she have a ring like this?"

The old man bent his head close to her hand, examining the class ring carefully with his weak eyes.

"That she did, young lady," he said. "That she did. But a feller can't be too careful. There was a man here a while back who claimed he was from that Wellington School for Girls." He stopped and looked around. "Had them Ewings running in circles, he did. But he didn't fool me. What would a man be doing working for a girls' school? I had him figured for a phony the minute I laid eyes on him."

Joan snickered. "That was Mr. Wharton," she said. "He's the president of our board of directors." But the bewhiskered stranger wasn't listening.

"You girls come over to my place by and by," he continued. "I've got something for ye. I want ye should take good care of it too. It's mighty important."

He turned and started to hobble away.

"But where do you live?" Gretchen called out.

"Around on t'other side of the pond," he said, without stopping or looking back. "Ye can find it easy. Just follow the trail as far as it goes. The cabin at the end, that's mine."

"We should have gone along with him," Gretchen said when he was out of sight. "Then we'd have been sure to find it."

"Oh, no!" Joan said, starting to turn toward the cabin. "We've got something else to do. Just before Old Whiskers turned up, I discovered that this window is unlocked." She reached up to open it. "I'm going in and see what's under that blanket."

Felicia hesitated uncertainly.

"Do–do you suppose that we ought to?" she asked.

"I don't know why not," Joan retorted. "That sideboard belongs to the school. It doesn't belong to the Ewings. And besides, we aren't going to take it. We're just going to look at it."

Before either of the others could protest, Joan pushed back the window and climbed inside. A moment later she squealed with delight.

"Come here, Felicia!" she cried. "It's the sideboard all right! It must be!"

She had flung the blanket aside to reveal the simple beauty of the massive piece of furniture.

Gretchen and Felicia both climbed through the window and stood beside the large chest. Felicia's breath was coming in short, quick gasps. Her whole body was trembling.

She reached out as though to touch the satin finish of the wood but drew back and stepped around to the other side. "It's beautiful," she breathed softly. "And it's like the Parker sideboard in Boston. Exactly. I'd recognize it anywhere."

"No wonder the Ewings wanted to get it out of there before we found it."

Felicia pulled open the drawer.

"It's the same kind of construction that was used in the other sideboard," she said. "See how smoothly these drawers pull,"

"But where is the proof that it's a Parker?" Joan asked. "Surely nobody will buy the thing and pay very much for it unless there's some sort of written proof that it's authentic."

"That's right," Felicia said. "But there shouldn't be any question about this. It certainly looks authentic, all right."

She looked over the sideboard carefully, exclaiming over the care with which it was made and the superlative beauty of the finish. Finally, she stopped and wrinkled her nose.

"Do you smell anything funny?" she asked.

Joan shook her head. "I don't smell anything."

"Neither do I," Gretchen said. "It's just the stale, musty smell of the cabin."

"That isn't what I smell," Felicia persisted. "Something smells like fresh oil to me."

"Fresh oil?" Joan scoffed. "This piece of furniture was made over two hundred years ago. Remember?"

"I know," the young Christian said, "but something smells awfully strange to me. My aunt does a lot of refinishing and that sort of thing at her antique shop, and she uses an oil that smells exactly like that."

"You're imagining it," Joan scoffed again. "This sideboard looks older than anything I've ever seen in the way of furniture. It wouldn't be smelling of fresh oil."

Felicia stepped back and looked at the chest again, critically. "It is beautiful," she said, "but that odor still bothers me."

"We'd better be getting out of here," Gretchen said. "What if Herman starts to look for us and catches us in here?"

Felicia started toward the door when she saw a large wooden box beneath the table in the opposite corner of the cabin. She went over and pulled it out so she could look into it.

"I wonder what this is?" she asked. "Maybe that smell of fresh oil comes from here."

"Don't you recognize a box of tools when you see

it?" Gretchen said. "That's just like the toolbox my grandfather used to have."

The box was unlocked, and Felicia opened it. There were woodworking tools of every size and description – tiny wood chisels and draw knives, planes and squares and saws.

"Just look at those tools!" Joan exclaimed. "I didn't know they had so many tools outside of a hardware store."

There was a faint noise outside. The girls leaped to their feet instantly.

"What was that?" Gretchen asked.

They heard it again.

Joan laughed a moment later. "It's just a chipmunk," she said. "We're really getting jumpy."

"Just the same," Felicia answered, "we'd better be getting out of here. There's no telling when Herman will decide we ought to be home and come to look for us."

She shoved the heavy box of tools back under the table, and the three girls hurried out of the window, being careful to close it again and to leave everything just as they had found it.

CHAPTER 8

THE MISSING BIBLE

I don't see why we're going to see Old Whiskers," Joan said as they left the cabin and started along the shore of the pond toward the old man's cabin. "We know where the sideboard is. Why don't we call Mr. Wharton? He can take care of everything from here on out."

"Oh, we can't do that yet," Felicia replied. "We haven't got any evidence that this is the sideboard that Miss Grainger left to the school. There isn't anything yet to prove that it's any different from any other piece of antique furniture."

"And besides," Gretchen put in, "you know how skeptical Miss Duncan was. If we don't have absolute proof that the sideboard is the one that belongs to the school and is actually worth quite a lot of money, nobody would pay any attention to us."

"You know, the proof that that sideboard is a

genuine Parker is the whole key now," Joan said. "Maybe that's what Miss Grainger left with Jasper Denton. That would be something extremely important. And you know how Old Whiskers stressed that."

"I can tell you this much," Gretchen added. "Whatever we do, we've got to do it quickly. There are only a few more days left until that sideboard will legally belong to the Ewings. Then it won't make any difference what we find out about the sideboard and who actually made it."

The old man was waiting for them in front of his neat little cabin. He was sitting on the stoop with his cane in his hands, his pale blue eyes watery and more sunken than ever. When he saw the girls coming, he got to his feet and hobbled to meet them.

"I–I had it when I looked last week," he murmured as they approached. "I had it out and looked at it. But them Ewings must have sneaked in and stolen it." His bony fingers were quivering on the cane.

"What do you mean?" Felicia asked him.

"All that time they been messing around here, I should have known they'd pull something like that. I should have run them off the first time I seen them."

"What happened?" Joan asked excitedly.

"Miss Martha," he went on. "She told me to keep it until you came." He swallowed hard and mopped at his forehead with the back of his gnarled old hand. "And I did keep it until they came messing around. I thought I had it hid good, but it's gone! Those Ewings stole it!"

The girls looked at one another.

"What–what was it?" Gretchen asked at last.

"She told me it was awful important," he quavered. "She gave me that Bible herself and said, 'Now, Jasper, you see that the people from the college get this. And don't give it to anybody else. Don't even tell anybody else about it.' But them Ewings found out about it some way, and now it's gone!"

"A Bible?" Joan echoed. "Did I understand you to say that Miss Grainger gave you a Bible to keep for the school authorities?"

The old fellow nodded miserably.

"What could be so important about a Bible?" Gretchen asked, disappointment in her voice. "You know how Miss Grainger was about salvation and that sort of thing. Maybe she thought it would be a good chance to preach to somebody."

But Joan shook her head. "It's something more than that," she said.

"You're thinking the same thing I am," Felicia said, taking her friend by the arm and squeezing it. "The Ewings were reading a Bible when we got home yesterday afternoon. Remember how they were sitting there, poring over it, and didn't even hear us come in?"

"And how mad they got!" Joan finished.

"I knowed it!" Jasper rasped between clenched

teeth. "I just knowed they was the ones that got it! When I first saw that it was gone, I knowed!"

"I don't see that there's anything for us to get so alarmed about," Gretchen put in. "I still think Miss Grainger was more interested in getting us to read the Bible than anything else. You know how she was, Joan. She was like Felicia here, always trying to make Christians out of everybody. Probably thought it was a good chance to get somebody to read the Bible carefully."

Joan's face was solemn.

"I don't know that there's anything so terrible about that, Gretchen," she said, her voice rising. "I haven't become a Christian yet, but I certainly don't make fun of anyone who has."

"Well," the other girl retorted quickly, "you don't need to get so huffy about it."

"I think this particular Bible has another meaning," Felicia said quietly. "I'm sure that Miss Grainger wasn't thinking only of witnessing to someone when she left that Bible with Mr. Denton and asked him to be sure that someone from Wellington got it. I'm positive that it has something to do with that sideboard."

"But how could it?" Gretchen persisted.

Felicia was silent a moment.

"I don't know," she said. "But that's something we'll have to figure out. Right now we've got to find a way to get hold of that Bible. It should have the information in it that would prove whether this sideboard is a genuine Parker or not. At least the Ewings must think it has something to do with it."

"I suppose it could be," Gretchen answered doubtfully. "But it hardly seems likely to me."

"We'll have to get hold of it and see."

"That's not going to be so easy," Joan answered. "They didn't even want us to see it. I don't know how we'll manage to get our hands on it."

"Just the same," Felicia said, "I've got an idea if you two will just help me."

"I'd like to get my hands on them," Jasper Denton muttered darkly. "I'd just like to get hold of them for about three minutes. I'd make them sorry they ever showed up around my place."

* * *

Herman and Clarissa Ewing were sitting in the kitchen when the girls entered the house for dinner that evening. Herman was sitting quietly at the table, and Clarissa was working at the cupboard. Dinner was almost ready.

"Well," Herman asked, "did you find your sideboard today?"

Felicia colored delicately.

Gretchen said, "We did do a lot of exploring."

"It's a good thing you didn't get lost," he answered. "We don't like to have you wandering around in the forest like that. There's no telling what kind of trouble you can get into. We might have to get the whole countryside out to look for you."

"Oh," Joan answered easily, "we always stay on the main trails. We don't go back into the woods at all. We'd just as soon walk out along the highway."

"Maybe you've given up finding that sideboard, eh?" His eyes narrowed slightly as the question was blurted out.

"It certainly isn't in the house," Felicia answered. "We would have found it if it had been."

"Well now, I knew that was the way it would be," Herman went on. "But you'll feel more satisfied now that you've looked for yourself. And I know the school authorities will be too."

"You know, Mrs. Ewing," Joan said when the woman was setting the table, "I'd like to have some more of that delicious blueberry jam. Did you make it yourself?"

Clarissa smiled warmly and turned toward the kitchen door. "Herman helped me pick the berries, but I used a special recipe of my own. You just wait here. I'll go down to the cellar and get another jar."

The moment she was gone, Joan turned her attention to Herman. As she began to talk excitedly to him, Felicia got up and sauntered into the living room. Ewing didn't even notice that she was gone.

"Now where could that Bible be?" she asked herself. "The bookcase was open. It could be over there. Or on the desk that stood on one side of the great fireplace. It might even be in their bedroom. Or perhaps – There it was! On the mantel!"

With a quick glance out toward where the others were sitting, she got the Bible down and began to look at it. It was a very old Book and gave every evidence of having been read countless times. There were pages that were loose and others that were tattered and dog-eared.

But for all of that, it was a very ordinary Bible. Why would she want them to have it? What was there about it that was so important as far as the sideboard was concerned? She began to leaf through the pages hurriedly. It could be that she had the wrong Bible, or–

She was looking so intently at the Book that she did not hear Joan cough loudly or Gretchen call to her.

"Felicia!" Gretchen called loudly. "Felicia, come here!"

She did not even hear Herman Ewing step into the room.

"What are you doing?" he snarled angrily.

Felicia was petrified at the sound of his voice. She was so startled that she dropped the Bible on the floor!

CHAPTER 9

WORKING ON CLUES

What have you got there?" Herman Ewing demanded harshly.

Felicia's face was flaming. "I–I was looking at this Bible," she stammered, stooping to pick up the Book. Her hands were trembling, and she could feel the color that flamed up in her face and the back of her neck.

"What were you doing with that Bible anyway?" Herman demanded angrily. "Who gave you permission to touch it?"

As she picked up the Bible a small piece of paper and one of the leaves fluttered out.

"Now look what you've done," Herman snorted, making a dive for the leaf that had fallen from the Bible.

Hurriedly Felicia stepped on the piece of paper, looking up to see if Herman Ewing had noticed it.

But he had eyes only for the Bible. He snatched up the page and wrenched the Bible from her hands.

"What were you doing with this anyway?" he asked again. "Who told you that you could touch it?"

"It's such an interesting looking Bible," she told him, "that I wanted to look at it. Did it belong to Miss Grainger too?"

"I guess it did belong to the old lady," Herman said, cooling a little. "I don't think me and Clarissa ever owned one."

By this time Joan and Gretchen had come into the living room.

"But this is the strangest Bible I've ever seen," he went on, opening it. "Can't make heads or tails of it. Me and Clarissa sat there for hours reading it, but it don't make sense."

"What do you mean?" Joan asked. "Aren't all Bibles alike?"

"Not this one," he grumbled. "Just look at it." He opened it to the book of John. "Look at the way Miss Grainger marked it all up. Got different verses marked all the way through the Bible. And I just can't make heads or tails to any of it."

While he was talking, Felicia slipped the sheet of paper into her pocket.

"You know," Herman went on, with a sudden reversal of mood, "this Book is mighty interesting to read, at that. I got to reading it last night. And, you know, there's some things in here that I never knew before. And things I had trouble understanding too. Now you take this here reference, for instance, 'All we like sheep have gone astray.' That's marked in red."

A strange look came into Herman's eyes.

"You know," he went on, "that makes a person think when he comes to stuff like that. It sure does. It–"

The kitchen door opened, and Clarissa Ewing came stomping in. She took in the situation at a glance.

"Herman Ewing," she exclaimed from the sitting room door, "why have you got that Bible?"

He grinned sheepishly and closed it. "The girls were just looking at it," he said. "That's all."

"You know that that Bible belonged to my dear, departed cousin," Clarissa said, snatching it from him and starting toward the bedroom. "We can't have anything happen to it."

"But nothing was going to happen to it, Clarissa," he protested. "We were just looking at it."

"Well," she snapped, "look at something else."

Herman grinned at the girls awkwardly in the silence that followed. "I don't know why I want to mess around looking at that," he said offhandedly. "I can't understand it anyway. Now, if it had been one of my woodworking journals, I could probably figure it out. But I couldn't make heads or tails out of that Bible."

Woodworking journal! Felicia started, remembering the tools in the old cabin and the smell of fresh oil.

"Are–are you a wood carver, Mr. Ewing?" she asked, trying to sound innocent.

He hesitated, instantly alert and suspicious.

"What makes you ask that?" he asked her.

"You just mentioned a woodworking journal," she said. "I wondered if you were a wood carver." He shook his head vigorously.

"Not me," he said. "I hardly know enough about wood to build a fire. Nope, all I've ever done all my life is farm."

When Mrs. Ewing came back into the room, the girls went into the kitchen and ate in almost complete silence. And as soon as they finished, they went directly to their room.

"You know," Felicia began, "I think Herman Ewing was lying when he said that he wasn't a wood carver."

Gretchen looked up at her.

"What difference does that make?" she asked.

"I don't know," Felicia said slowly. "It might make a lot of difference. It might not make any. It just seems strange that he should lie about it, that's all."

For several minutes Felicia and Gretchen sat there talking. They didn't notice that Joan wasn't entering into the conversation until she said, "What does this mean, Felicia?"

Felicia looked up to see that Joan had her Bible and was reading it.

"Do you mean to tell me that you're falling for

that?" Gretchen laughed. "That would be an even bigger joke than having Felicia go religious."

Joan did not answer her.

"What does this mean, Felicia?" she asked again. "It says that Jesus said no one can see the kingdom of God unless they are born again. Now what does that mean?"

"Why do you ask?" the Christian girl wanted to know.

"It was one of the verses that was underlined in Miss Grainger's Bible," Joan went on. "I noticed that when Herman was showing it to us. It sounded so funny that I wondered what it meant."

"That's one of the verses that tells us that we all must make a decision concerning Christ," Felicia answered, carefully choosing her words. "You know, the Bible tells us that we all have sinned and fallen short of the glory of God, that none of us is righteous." She paused a moment.

"Or like that verse that Herman was asking about tonight, we are told that we've all sinned, like sheep who have gone astray. The Bible tells us too, that only God is holy, and Christ, who came and lived a sinless life here on earth."

Joan leaned forward, listening intently. The color was gone from her face, and her gaze was riveted on Felicia. Gretchen, who had been listening in spite of herself, coughed nervously and rattled her magazine.

"And a little farther along in this chapter," Felicia

went on, "we are told that the only way we can have eternal life is to trust the Lord Jesus Christ as our personal Savior. That we must confess our sins and put our whole trust in Him."

"I don't think I ever heard anything like that before," Joan said seriously. "Somehow I had the idea that this being a Christian was a lot of don'ts. I thought that a person had to be a spoilsport and never have any fun if he was going to follow Christ."

"Nothing is farther from the truth," Felicia said. "Of course, there are certain things that it is better for a Christian not to do. But being a Christian isn't a matter of 'don't do this' and 'don't do that.' It's a matter of loving Christ and putting our whole trust in Him to save us and to keep us from sin."

Gretchen put aside her magazine and got noisily to her feet.

"Felicia," she broke in abruptly, "what was that piece of paper that you picked up? The one that fell out of the Bible?"

"Why, I'd forgotten all about it," Felicia said, digging into her pocket. "It's probably just a piece of paper the Ewings were using for a marker. I don't know why I stepped on it and picked it up. It just seemed like the thing to do at the time."

The girls began to examine the paper carefully.

"That isn't in Clarissa's handwriting," Joan said. "She uses big, bold strokes. I remember when she made out the receipt for our room deposit."

Felicia looked over her shoulder. "Why, that looks like Miss Grainger's handwriting," she said. "You remember how she had written in the margins of her Bible. She had that same dainty style."

Gretchen took the paper and studied it for a moment.

"That is Miss Grainger's handwriting," she exclaimed. "I'd recognize it anywhere."

"Do you suppose that piece of paper has been in the Bible all the time?"

"2 Timothy 2:20," Felicia read. Then she stopped and straightened suddenly. "I just thought of something," she said. "This could be what she wanted Jasper to give us. It might be a code that would tell us something about the sideboard!"

She took the Bible and began to open it, her hands trembling with excitement as she fumbled with the pages.

"What does it say?" Joan asked.

"'But in a great house,'" she read, "'there are not only vessels of gold and of silver, but also of wood. . . .'"

"Did you hear that?" Gretchen cried. "That's it! That must have reference to the sideboard."

"It must mean that the sideboard is in the big house," Felicia said. "There couldn't be any other meaning."

"It was in the old house," Joan said laconically. "It's stored down in the old cabin by the pond, remember?"

But Felicia was already fumbling with the Bible

again. "Just a minute," she said. "Let's get this second reference. 1 Thessalonians 5:5." She almost dropped the Bible in her haste to find the verse.

"It says that you are all children of light and children of the day. We are not of the night nor of the darkness."

Joan ran her fingers through her short hair.

"What could that possibly mean?" she asked. "There isn't anything in this that would give us a clue."

Felicia thought for a moment.

"The first verse is plain enough," she said. "The treasure is in the house. So, starting with that, what room in the house would be the room of light?"

"That big sitting room with the fireplace!" Gretchen exclaimed tensely, her eyes lighting. "It's the room with the most light and the room that is used the most in the daytime. Do–do you suppose that could be it?"

"It sounds logical enough," Felicia agreed. She examined the scrap of paper intently. "But it looks as though there's another reference here, but it's been torn out. I can't just make out the *J*."

"What book in the Bible starts with a *J*?" Joan asked.

"Oh, that could be John," Felicia said, "or Joshua or Jeremiah or another book."

"Well," Joan said, her voice revealing her disappointment, "we couldn't just leaf through all the books beginning with *J* and find it." She was biting her lower lip thoughtfully.

"That would be the most important clue too," Felicia

went on. "It's the one that will give us the location of the sideboard or whatever it is this code is about."

"I don't know," Joan replied, "whether this thing means all that or not. There isn't any place in the sitting room that's big enough to hide that sideboard. Besides, we know where it is already."

"Herman and Clarissa know where it is too," Felicia reminded her. "And they're desperately searching through the Bible too. It could be that the code isn't about the sideboard itself. Maybe Miss Grainger made it to give us the location of the proof we would have to have to establish the sideboard as authentic."

Gretchen, who hadn't been taking part in the conversation, looked up. "I just thought of something," she said. "I saw a little piece of paper like this on the floor in the kitchen just before dinner this evening. Mrs. Ewing threw it in the wastebasket."

"Are you sure?" Felicia asked.

"If she did," Joan said, "it's probably been burned by now. Herman emptied the wastebasket right after dinner."

Gretchen picked up the flashlight and started for the door. "We've got to find out," she said. "I'm going to check the trash barrel."

Felicia and Joan joined her.

"We're going to have to be awfully quiet," Gretchen whispered. "We don't want Herman and Clarissa to know what we're up to. Perhaps it would be better if I went alone."

Reluctantly the other two turned back. In a few short moments Gretchen came tiptoeing up the stairs.

"Did you find it?" they asked excitedly. "Did you find it?"

For answer she held up a magazine triumphantly. "I found this," she announced, "with Herman Ewing's name on it. The latest issue of the *Woodworker's Journal.*"

"Then he was lying to us about his trade," said Felicia.

"But why would he do that?" Joan asked, wrinkling her forehead.

"There's only one reason that I can think of," Felicia replied. "I think he made an imitation of that Parker sideboard with the idea of selling it as the original."

Joan and Gretchen looked at her quizzically. "Then, you mean the one in the cabin is a fake?"

"That's what I think. The smell of fresh oil and the woodworking tools and now this information that Herman Ewing is a carver by trade all fit together."

"It does make sense," Joan said hesitantly, "but I can't see why he'd be so interested in finding the real sideboard if he had already made an imitation that was good enough to pass as an original."

"If the original existed, he'd have to find it if he could," Felicia went on. "If someone else found it, it would ruin his whole plan and maybe put him in the pen too."

"You make a good Sherlock," Gretchen said, smiling broadly. "Now let's see what you can do with this." She held up a scrap of paper. "It says here, Joel 2:16."

"Joel 2:16," Felicia repeated. "Here, hand me my Bible."

Her hands were trembling so that she could scarcely turn the pages.

"Let me have that," Joan said with some degree of calmness. "Where is it? In the Old or New Testament?"

"I've got it now," Felicia told her. "I can't make much out of the first part of the verse, and I certainly don't see how the last could mean anything. . . . Let the bridegroom go forth of his chamber, and the bride out of her closet,'" she read slowly. "What could that possibly mean?"

Gretchen took the Bible and read the verse herself.

"I don't know," she answered, shaking her head. "Maybe Miss Grainger had to give a talk somewhere and used these three verses. We could be making a terrible blunder."

Felicia disagreed.

"We might not be figuring it out right," she said, "but I'm convinced that those verses have reference to the sideboard in some way. They couldn't be part of a speech. They don't have any central theme."

"I wouldn't know about that," Gretchen said sharply. "I'm not an authority on sermons as you are."

"Maybe," Joan said thoughtfully, "we could get the Ewings out of the way tomorrow. Then we could go down into the sitting room and examine it carefully with those verses in mind."

CHAPTER 10

UNRAVELING THE CODE

The girls scarcely slept that night, and in the morning at the breakfast table, Herman Ewing chided them.

"What sort of a party were the three of you at last night?" he asked. "You look as sleepy as I do."

"What sort of a party were you at?" Joan countered.

"I'd never tell that," he said, grinning.

Clarissa frowned disapprovingly at him.

"You girls are welcome to stay as long as you wish," she said a moment later, her voice chilled and incisive. "But I would like to know about how long you are going to be with us. It requires a certain amount of preparation, and with all the work Herman and I have to do, we would just as soon be alone."

Felicia looked at Joan and Gretchen.

"Oh, you won't need to worry about us," Joan said

easily. "We'll be going back in a few days. We'll have to be in school next Monday."

Clarissa Ewing sighed audibly and brushed her hair from her forehead.

Herman held his coffee cup for her to fill. "What do you girls plan on doing today?" he asked.

Felicia swallowed hard and took a deep breath.

"We thought that we'd fool around this morning," she said, "but this afternoon I'd like to go back to that little cabin in the woods."

"What cabin?" Herman asked quickly, fear flashing like a signal in his eyes.

"Why the one down by that pond," she said innocently. "We saw the cutest little cabin down there when we were out walking the other day. I haven't said anything to the other girls, but I thought it would be nice to go back and see what it's like. There's a big chest in there or something."

Herman dropped his fork and stared up at her. Clarissa Ewing turned quickly, the spatula in her hand.

"I wouldn't monkey around that cabin this morning if I were you," Herman said shortly. "There's an old fellow who lives out that way who's sorta crazy. There's no telling what he might do."

"Oh, I don't think Mr. Denton would hurt us," Felicia continued. "We had a nice long visit with him. He said that he used to work for Miss Grainger. He's a very interesting man. We call him Old Whiskers."

Herman Ewing was staring angrily at the girls.

"I said that you'd better not monkey around that cabin," he snapped. "It just ain't safe."

Felicia shrugged her shoulders.

"Oh, I guess it isn't that important to us," she said. "But we did get to wondering about what that big object is doing out there. And it's got a brand-new padlock on the door too. That seemed so strange to us."

Joan kicked her on the ankle and shook her head in warning. Gretchen, too, was scowling darkly.

"I wish that you girls would do something for me this morning," Clarissa put in a few minutes later. "We're expecting a very important phone call here at the house, and Mr. Ewing and I have an errand to do that just can't be put off. Do you suppose you could stay here and answer the phone for us? You can take the message as well as we can."

Felicia turned to her companions. "I think we could do that, don't you?" she asked.

"It's up to you," Joan told her. "You seem to be doing all the talking this morning."

Herman had taken two eggs and four strips of bacon and had begun to eat hungrily. But when the conversation turned to the little cabin in the woods, he suddenly lost his appetite. He drank his coffee hurriedly and got to his feet.

"Well, Clarissa," he said, reaching for his hat, "are you ready to go now?"

"Just as soon as I get my sweater."

With that the two of them hurried out, got into the pickup truck, and went jouncing away.

"Now why did you do that?" Joan turned on Felicia almost angrily. "Why did you let them know that we had found out about the sideboard down in that old cabin? Now they'll move it, and we never will find it again."

"And time means everything now," Gretchen added. "We've only got another forty hours to find the genuine Parker and prove that it's authentic."

"That's exactly what I was thinking of," Felicia answered. "It was the only way I could think of to get rid of them so that we could go over the house and try to unravel the code and find the true Parker."

"Well," Joan said practically, "we'd better get at it. There's no telling when Herman and Clarissa will be back."

The three girls stood together in the doorway of the big, high-ceilinged sitting room, looking about uncertainly.

"I don't know where to start," Gretchen said at last. "I think we've figured out the first two clues correctly. That would trace the sideboard to the sitting room. But this last one is terrible. I don't see where we could get any bride's closets in here or any bridegroom's chambers."

They walked around the room, examining each inch of wall space.

"This house reminds me somewhat of the one

my great-aunt used to live in," Joan said. "It had a big fireplace like this with a nice, big china closet on one side of it. My relatives had closed up one of those secret staircases that were built in so many of these old houses so the early settlers would have a place to hide from Indian raids. The china closet swung out to let them in from the living-room end of the staircase.

"That's it!" Felicia cried excitedly, staring at the massive old fireplace and the expanse of wall that surrounded it. "That's it!"

"What do you mean?" asked Joan.

"Look at the wallpaper on that wall," Felicia answered, pointing to the side of the room with the fireplace. "It's a lighter shade than the rest of the paper, and the pattern is slightly different. That means that it was papered either before or after the rest of the room."

"But I don't see what that has to do with it," Gretchen said.

"Some of those old staircases were disguised with unsightly wood boxes beside the fireplace," Felicia continued. "If that was the case here, the people might have filled it in with wallboard or lathe and plaster."

CHAPTER 11

UNDER THE SECRET STAIRS

They're coming!" Joan cried again. "They're coming! What are we going to do?"

"Quick!" Gretchen exclaimed, starting for the stairs. "We've got to get out of here! We can't let them catch us!"

The two were already on the stairs, but Felicia was still working at the fireplace, hurriedly running her fingers along the smoke-blackened bricks.

The jeep had slammed noisily to a stop.

"Come on, Felicia!" Joan whispered tensely. "We've got to get out of here. If they catch us, it'll ruin everything!"

The kitchen door opened loudly, and they heard the sound of feet hurrying across the floor.

"It's too late!" Gretchen gasped.

"Miss Bailey!" they heard Clarissa Ewing call,

her voice shrill and high. "Miss Cartright! Where are you?"

Felicia, who had been exploring the inside of the fireplace, touched a small indentation.

"I–I think I've found it!" she exclaimed.

She pressed the lever and the panel next to the fireplace swung open, revealing a narrow, dark, twisting passageway.

"Look!"

"Hurry!" Felicia ordered. "We've got to get inside!"

They were not an instant too soon. They heard footsteps on the regular staircase as they clambered into the secret stairs and pushed the paneling shut. Even as it swung into place, they heard the door to the room open. Clarissa and Herman came in.

"I know they're in here," Clarissa said, her voice trembling. "They've got to be in the house somewhere! Their car is outside!"

"Maybe they took a shortcut to the cabin," Herman said. "I tell you, we should have gone over there and got that sideboard moved to a place where they wouldn't be able to find it. If the school authorities claim it, the whole six months' work will be ruined."

"All we've got to do is to keep those girls here until tomorrow night," Clarissa countered icily. "You know that. Then the sideboard will be ours. We won't have a thing to worry about."

"No," he said, "nothing to worry about except being able to palm that sideboard off as the original.

Nothing to worry about except trying to fool some of the best experts in the country. I wish we could have found that code in the Bible we stole from old man Denton. I'd feel a lot better about the whole affair."

"So would I," his wife answered nervously. "I thought when we found that slip of paper with those verses written on that we had it, but we couldn't make heads or tails of them."

"She was such a religious fanatic that she had scraps of paper with Bible verses on them all over the house," Herman said. "No, sir, that Bible is it. The code is hidden among those verses she underlined if we could just figure it out."

"I suppose you're right," his wife answered. "It must tell where she's hidden the proof that the original sideboard was made by Abner Parker. That's the only thing that I can figure."

"It could tell where the original sideboard is hidden too," he told her. "If we could find it, we wouldn't have to take a chance with my imitation."

"We've turned this house upside down," she said, "and neither the sideboard nor any reference to it is around. If it weren't for the will and what we've heard the relatives say, I'd even doubt that the thing existed at all."

"I don't know why that cousin of yours had to be so blasted cute," he lashed. "She could have left that sideboard out in plain sight."

"Maybe she knew what kind of a man I married,"

Clarissa retorted, "and wanted to be sure that the school would get it."

Herman swore angrily and stomped out the door.

"Well," he called from the hallway, "come on! We've got to get those girls before they get away from here!"

Felicia, Joan, and Gretchen crouched in the darkness on the other side of the heavy panel, scarcely daring to breathe. Their throats were constricted, and perspiration appeared on their foreheads. Felicia ran her fingers through her hair nervously. They didn't move or speak until at last they heard the Ewings storming through the other part of the house.

"What are we going to do?" Gretchen whispered in Felicia's ear. "We can't let them catch us!"

Felicia shook her head.

They were standing so close together that they could scarcely move.

"I know that," she said tensely. "But we can't leave now. They'd catch us before we got out of the house."

"Besides," Joan said determinedly, "I want to find out about that sideboard."

"If we could just see something in here," Gretchen remarked, "we might be able to find it. But it's so dark in here that I wouldn't dare try to go down these steep stairs."

"You've got that flashlight, haven't you?" Joan asked. "You've been carrying it with you everywhere we've gone."

Herman and Clarissa were going over the house

for a second time, calling loudly first for one of the girls and then another. They came back through the upstairs bedroom again. Gretchen, Joan, and Felicia huddled together without speaking.

"Have you got that flashlight?" Joan asked when the Ewings were gone again.

"I've got it," Gretchen said, "but we don't dare turn it on, do we? If they see a light shining from under the panel, they'll have us."

"I don't think any light could escape to give us away," Joan said. "Didn't you notice how tightly those panels were fitted? The Ewings have lived here for months and haven't seen it."

Gretchen hesitated a moment, then switched on the flashlight, and shone it down the narrow, twisting stairs.

"Do–do you suppose we dare go down?" she whispered.

"We aren't going to stop this close to unraveling that code," Joan announced firmly, pushing ahead and taking the flashlight.

They went down the steep staircase step by step, clinging to the rough mortar and bricks as the stairs wound about the chimney. At the bottom, the opening widened to reveal a small room. And there under the stairs was a huge walnut chest, thickly coated with dust!

"Felicia!" Joan gasped when she saw it. For the moment she could say no more.

Felicia and Gretchen stood where they were, staring wide-eyed. They could see at a glance that it was beautiful, an almost exact duplicate of the one that was in the little cabin, even to the intricate pulls on the drawers and the design on the little molding along the top.

"That's it!" the Christian girl said softly, reaching out a trembling hand to touch the exquisite piece of furniture. "That's the sideboard Miss Grainger left to the school!"

She touched the drawers. They opened as smoothly and as quietly as though they had been made yesterday. Although the sideboard was more than two hundred years old, the drawers opened as effortlessly as those on the sideboard that Herman had just made.

"We've found it!" Joan breathed excitedly.

"Shh!" Felicia whispered. "Herman and Clarissa are still looking for us. Remember?"

They were silent for an instant or two.

"Now," Joan said, "if we can just find the proof that it's authentic!"

"That code Miss Grainger left would prove that the sideboard is old, all right," Felicia said, "and that it belonged to Miss Grainger, but we'll have to find a bill of sale or a statement in Abner Parker's handwriting to prove that it is authentic."

They opened first one drawer and then another, but there was no sign of any paper or anything else, for that matter. With Puritan thoroughness, Miss

Grainger, or her mother, had cleaned the drawers spotlessly.

"It isn't here," Felicia said, after a minute or two.

"Let me look," Gretchen said. "Sometimes papers get shoved in behind drawers. We've had that happen at home several times."

She took three drawers out of the sideboard while Joan and Felicia watched. There were a few scraps of paper, an old comb, and a pin of some sort that was broken and very, very old.

As Gretchen pulled the fourth drawer from the sideboard she gasped. There, crumpled back of the drawer, was a yellowed slip of paper, wrinkled, and brittle with age.

"I've found it!" she exclaimed softly. Her hands were quivering as she took it and looked at it.

Joan and Felicia both tried to read over her shoulder, but she turned away from them.

"Look! 'I hereby sell to Jonas Parker, one sideboard in exchange for two pigs and one suckling calf. June 17, 1772. Signed, Abner Parker.'"

"The bill of sale!" Felicia cried. "There's the evidence that we've been looking for!"

They stared at one another tensely, scarcely daring to move. Felicia shivered.

"What are we going to do now?" she asked.

"We've got to sneak out of here and make a call," Joan said, "just as quickly as we can."

"Maybe we can get out and get the car," Gretchen

whispered. "If we could do that, we could get into town away from the Ewings and call Mr. Wharton. He'd know what to do next."

They had slowly climbed up the steep staircase when Clarissa and Herman Ewing came back into the sitting room not a dozen feet away from them.

"I tell you, Clarissa, they're not back at the cabin!" Herman stormed. "I just checked it! Now quit yelling at me about that!"

"Then they're still in the house somewhere. They've got to be."

"I know! I know!" Herman told her. "They've got to be! That's what you've been saying for the last hour. But where? Just tell me that!"

"Don't just stand there! Go out and do something to their car. We can't let them get away now!" screamed Clarissa.

"That's the first sensible thing you've said all day."

"That settles it," Joan whispered when the Ewings had gone outside. "We'll have to get somewhere our phones will work and call Mr. Wharton."

"But how?"

"We'll have to wait until they get to sleep," Joan said. "Then we can sneak out and get up to that gas station four or five miles up the road."

"I–I suppose that's the only thing we can do," Felicia agreed.

For an hour or more they sat on the steps, talking little.

"Get me that Bible again, Clarissa," they heard Herman Ewing call angrily from the kitchen. "I'm going to figure out that blasted code or know the reason why."

"Don't yell at me that way!"

"I still think those verses on that piece of paper meant something," Herman told her, "even if you don't. I'd like to know what happened to it. It was in the Bible yesterday."

"You don't suppose they got it?" his wife asked. "You know, you showed it to them."

"Showed it to them, nothing!" he declared, his voice rising. "They sneaked in and got it. That's what happened!"

There was a short silence.

"Herman, that's it!" Clarissa said, her voice breaking with excitement. "That's exactly what happened! They were acting so strangely this morning, trying to get us out of the house and everything. They must have found that slip of paper in the Bible and pocketed it. Then they figured out that code and found the sideboard!"

"Well, don't stand there like a ninny, woman! Get that Bible. I wrote those verse references down on the flyleaf. If those girls can figure out that code, so can we. Hurry!"

"What—what do you think now?" Felicia asked, her voice breaking.

"We'll just have to take a chance that they don't

get it figured out," Joan said. "There isn't anything else that we can do."

She was silent for a long while. Clarissa and Herman had come back into the sitting room, and the girls could hear them.

"'Children of light,'" the man said for the fourth time. "I wonder what that could mean. . . . Do you suppose they would belong in the room of light? What would be the room of light in this house?"

"The room with the most windows, of course," Clarissa answered dourly, "but I don't see–"

"We're in the room with the most windows right now," Herman said, his voice crescendoing. "And more light too."

"I don't see why we couldn't figure that out before," his wife answered quickly. "That makes real sense when you stop to think of it. But where could the sideboard be hidden in here?"

"We'd better look up the rest of these references." There was a short silence. "This Bible sort of interests me. Especially those verses about 'being born again.' I wonder what they mean," Herman kept on talking.

"Now don't start that," Clarissa retorted hotly. "I've had enough trouble with you ever since you started reading this Bible."

"I can't help it," her husband said. "Those verses that are marked get your attention, somehow. What do you suppose it means to be 'born again'?"

"Oh, stop it!" came Clarissa's answer, her temper rising, as they again left the room.

Joan, who had been sitting beside Felicia, turned toward her in the darkness.

"I feel the same way that Herman does, Felicia," she whispered. "I was lying awake half the night just thinking of the things you said to me about the Lord."

"It doesn't do too much good just to think about Jesus," Felicia told her, "unless you go all the way, confessing your sin, and putting your trust in Him to save you. Just thinking about Him isn't going to make any difference."

"What do you mean by being 'born again'?" Joan continued.

"It's really a very simple thing," Felicia replied. "We're supposed to confess our sins and put our trust in Christ. It's just like being born a second time. We're supposed to be new creatures."

"I don't get it at all," Joan answered.

"It's really a very simple thing. At first, we're sinful. The Bible tells us that we 'all have sinned, and come short of the glory of God.' And that the wages of sin are death. There are a good many verses like that in the Scriptures, Joan. When we accept Christ as our Savior, we confess that we are sinners and need someone to save us. Then we must put our trust in the Lord Jesus. That's what being 'born again' means," explained Felicia.

Joan was biting her lower lip.

"It's very much like driving down the wrong road," Felicia went on, choosing her words carefully. "You're on the wrong road. After a while you realize it. You stop and turn around to head in the right direction. That's almost what we do when we trust Christ as our Savior. We've been following Satan. Then we stop and turn around and follow the Lord."

"But I never could live a good life," Joan protested. "I'm not built that way. I like having good times and doing what I want to do too well."

"None of us can live a good life in ourselves," Felicia told her. "God doesn't expect us to live a good life on our own. But He does say that if we put our trust in Him, He will help us to live the way we ought to."

Joan took a deep breath.

"Would–would you help me to pray, Felicia?" she asked hoarsely.

Gretchen laughed uncomfortably.

"I never thought I'd live to see this," she said.

But neither of the girls heard what she had said.

"Oh, heavenly Father," Joan prayed in her same direct way, "You know how I've been going the wrong way. You know that I've been trying to please myself without giving any thought to You or what You want me to do. Now I know that I'm a sinner and that I'm lost. Won't You come into my heart and save me?"

Her voice broke, and for a moment she could not go on. But when she finished praying, Felicia prayed too. She was still praying when they heard Herman and Clarissa come back into the sitting room. Their voices were loud and excited.

"I don't know what the bride's closet could be," Clarissa said loudly. "But I just remembered that the room right above the sitting room was Uncle Jonathan's study. He always went in there to do his work. That could be the bridegroom's chamber."

"If it is, we'll find it!"

By that time, they were starting up the stairs.

"What are we going to do?" Gretchen whispered, straightening.

The girls' hearts were hammering a fierce beat.

"Both of you get up to the top of the stairway," Joan ordered quietly. "Get your hands on the lever that opens that panel! As soon as you hear them run downstairs, get out of here! Make a dash for the window that opens out onto the porch!"

"But what about you?" Felicia demanded. "And what about the sideboard?"

"Don't worry about me!" Joan told her. "I'll be right behind you! And as for the sideboard, they won't be any closer to getting it than they are right now!"

The girls crouched tensely at the top of the stairs, waiting.

"There might be something around this fireplace," came Herman's voice. Seems as though I remember hearing something about things like that in some of these old houses. They used to use them as a place where they could hide from the Indians."

At that moment Joan banged loudly with her fists on the plastered wall at the bottom of the stairway.

"What was that?" Herman Ewing cried.

Joan banged again.

"Come on, Herman!" Clarissa shouted. "They're downstairs!"

"Hurry!" Herman cried. "Don't let them get away!"

As the frantic couple dashed downstairs, the two girls opened the panel and ran across the room. Joan was right behind them, stopping at the fireplace only long enough to close the panel. She reached the window as the other two scrambled out onto the roof of the porch.

"This way!" she whispered, starting down the vine-covered porch post. "Hurry! They'll hear us and be after us any minute!"

CHAPTER 12

THE REAL THING
ON THE TRUCK

In a moment or two the three girls were on the ground and running across the yard toward the forest.

"Joan!" they heard Clarissa call. "Gretchen! Where are you?"

"Don't just stand there, Clarissa!" Herman shouted angrily. "They're around here somewhere! We've got to get them! We can't let them spoil everything now."

The girls ran as fast as they could. They ran until their breath was coming in long, hard gasps, and their legs could run no more.

"Do you suppose they're still after us?" Felicia panted.

"They're after us, all right," Joan said. "But I don't think they know which way we went. Now to get to that gas station and call just as quickly as possible."

"We'll have to stay away from the highway," Gretchen observed. "The first thing Herman will do is drive along the road and try to find us. He'll surely think of that gas station. He knows the first thing we'll do is head there."

"I just thought of something," Felicia said suddenly. "You've noticed how Clarissa and Herman go everywhere together, haven't you? Why don't we sneak back and watch until they leave? Then one of us can slip in and use their phone."

Gretchen gasped. "You mean go right back in their own house?"

"It might be safer than trying to call from the station," replied Felicia.

"I never thought of that," Joan agreed, "but that's right. If we go to the station, we'll have a lot of explaining to do to the man who's working there."

While they stood there talking, they saw the dim light of the jeep go bouncing along the county road.

"There they go now," Joan said.

"But we don't know that they're together," Gretchen protested. "One of them might have stayed here to look for us."

"That's a chance we'll have to take," Joan answered firmly. "Come on, let's get back there and get our phone call made before that jeep gets back."

They turned back, pushing their way through the forest until they reached the little clearing again.

"The lights are still on," Gretchen whispered

uncertainly. "Do you suppose that means that Clarissa is still there?"

"They'd leave the lights on anyway," Joan told her. "Let's separate now. I'll go around this way, and you two go the other. Then if I get caught making the call, you can get to town and get help."

They approached the big house cautiously, inching forward, and darting from the protective hand of one shadow to another. But it wouldn't have been necessary. Both Clarissa and Herman were gone. Gretchen and Felicia crouched among the trees not far from the house, while Joan ran in to phone.

"Hello," she said excitedly, "this is most important. I want to leave a message for Dr. Wilber Wharton. I can't stay here and talk, but would you give him this message? Tell him that the girls found what they were looking for. Tell him they need him badly, that he should hurry up here

just as quickly as possible."

There was a short pause.

"I know it's strange," Joan pleaded, but it's very important. And don't call back here with a report. Just get him the message as soon as you can! It's awfully important!"

At that instant Felicia ran to the door.

"Joan!" she shouted. "They're coming back!"

"Now you remember the name," Joan instructed hurriedly, her gaze fastened on the doorway. "Dr. Wharton. Tell him that it's important. He's got to get up here right away!"

The jeep was a quarter of the way up the lane when Joan hung up the phone and dashed outside. Felicia and Gretchen had already hurried across the clearing into the woods, where they waited breathlessly for Joan to join them.

"Do you think they saw you?" Gretchen asked.

"I know they didn't," Joan told them. "And I think we got that message through to Dr. Wharton."

"We'll have to pray that we did," Felicia said.

They watched while Herman and Clarissa lurched to a stop and hurried back into the house.

"Now what are we going to do?" Gretchen asked, her voice weak and small.

"Why don't we go over and see Old Whiskers?" Joan wondered aloud. "He's a fine old man. I'm sure he'd put us up for the night."

"And they'd never think of finding us over there!"

"But what about Mr. Wharton?" Gretchen asked. "How will he find us?"

"We won't have to worry about that until morning," Joan said. "We can get to town or the filling station or someplace where he can find us. I'm not afraid of Herman and Clarissa in the daytime."

* * *

It was late the next evening when they finally got into the car with Mr. Wharton, after the truck had left the big Grainger house with the sideboard.

"I was glad I was home when you called," he said. "I got the state troopers on the phone, and they got out to the house just after the Ewings found the sideboard in its hiding place under that secret staircase."

"What will happen to them now?" Felicia asked.

"Nothing as far as the school is concerned," the man answered. "And I don't think the authorities are interested in holding them. They didn't get the chance to try to sell the faked sideboard, so there's no charge of attempted fraud facing them."

"That was fortunate for them," answered Felicia.

"The school is fortunate too," continued Mr. Wharton. "You girls have made it possible for us to think about the addition to the school library which we've been needing for so long. The money that we can get from the sale of this sideboard will give us the start we need toward it. I don't mind telling you how much we appreciate what you've done. You see, we had really given up on it when you came up here."

"If it hadn't been for Felicia, we would have given up on it ourselves," Gretchen replied.

Joan turned to Felicia, who was sitting beside her.

"If it hadn't been for you," she said softly, "something else wouldn't have happened. I wouldn't have found the Lord Jesus Christ as my Savior."

Felicia smiled at her happily.

THE
FELICIA CARTRIGHT
SERIES

Felicia Cartright, a petite blonde who is one of the most popular students at Wellington School for Girls, has a surprising inclination toward mysteries. If a mysterious situation arises, it either makes its way to Felicia, or Felicia somehow finds it. Though this is a bit trying for her happy-go-lucky roommate, Joan Bailey, it does prevent life from becoming monotonous. It also enables Bernard Palmer, the popular author of the "Danny Orlis" books, to write an entertaining series of stories for girls aged twelve to eighteen.

The mysteries range from a valuable missing antique to an attempt by claim jumpers to steal a deposit of tungsten ore. There's excitement and action galore—but there's also spiritual guidance and blessing because Felicia and her partner-in-adventure love the Lord and take Him into account in all their experiences.

AVAILABLE FROM WWW.ANEKOPRESS.COM